ENZO BIANCHI

ECHOES
of the
WORD

A New Kind of Monk on the Meaning of Life

Foreword by Jonathan Wilson-Hartgrove

PARACLETE PRESS
BREWSTER, MASSACHUSETTS

2013 First Printing This Edition

Echoes of the Word: A New Kind of Monk on the Meaning of Life

ISBN 978-1-61261-373-4

Translated by Christine Landau.
First published in Great Britain in 2002 by Society for Promoting Christian Knowledge, 36 Causton Street, London SW1P 4ST, www.spckpublishing.co.uk

Original Italian version published in 1999 as *Le parole della spiritualità: Per un lessico della vita interiore* by Rizzoli. Second edition published 2012. Copyright © Enzo Bianchi 2002, 2012

© 2013 Foreword by Jonathan Wilson-Hartgrove

Enzo Bianchi has asserted his right under the Copyright, Designs and Patents Act, 1988, to be identified as Author of this work.

This edition published by Paraclete Press, Brewster, Massachusetts, www.paracletepress .com.

Many of the Scripture quotations are taken from the New Revised Standard Version of the Bible, copyright © 1989 by the Division of Christian Education of the National Council of the Churches of Christ in the USA. Used by permission. All rights reserved.

Other translations of Scripture quotations are provided by the translator.

The Paraclete Press name and logo (dove on cross) are trademarks of Paraclete Press, Inc.

Library of Congress Cataloging-in-Publication Data
Bianchi, Enzo.
 [Parole della spiritualità. English]
 Echoes of the word : a new kind of monk on the meaning of life / Enzo Bianchi ; foreword by Jonathan Wilson-Hartgrove.
  pages cm
 Includes bibliographical references.
 ISBN 978-1-61261-373-4 (trade pbk.)
 1. Meditations. I. Title.
 BV4832.3.B5313 2013
 242—dc23   2013024327

10 9 8 7 6 5 4 3 2 1

Published by Paraclete Press
Brewster, Massachusetts
www.paracletepress.com
Printed in the United States of America

ENZO BIANCHI was born in Castel Boglione, Piedmont, Italy, in 1943. In 1965, after graduating from the University of Turin, he founded an ecumenical monastic community—the Bose Community—of which he is still the prior. A well-known author of books on *lectio divina* and the spiritual life, which have been translated into many languages, Fr. Bianchi has dedicated himself to the search for spirituality capable of giving vitality to Christians today and furthering communion among all people.

As one of the original centers of new monasticism in Europe, with important links to ancient monastic ways, the Bose Community currently includes eighty vowed brothers and sisters of various Christian traditions, and receives thousands of visitors annually.

CONTENTS

FOREWORD

Some years ago, when I was visiting my spiritual director at a Benedictine monastery, he said to me over lunch, "Are you busy tomorrow afternoon? I'd like you to meet my spiritual director." It turned out she was a Benedictine sister in her mid 90s who'd spent 30 years of her life as a hermit. I wasn't sure what to expect, but I trusted my director. He drove me to the care facility where this sister's community was helping her through her last years. We sat at a small circular table with three chairs and talked for an hour. Then my director and I got back in his car and returned to the monastery.

It was as simple as that, really. But that one hour from so many years ago sticks out in my memory as one of the times when I have felt the presence of God most clearly. It's also an experience that continues to make me long for a spiritual life that taps into the deep wells of God's mercy.

When I returned home from the monastery, I wrote a note to this amma whose aliveness to God had so inspired me. I wanted to thank her for taking the time to share with me. Several weeks later, I got a note back from one of her sisters. In the week or so between our visit and my letter, she had died. But she had, just days before, been so alive—so present to me in every way. What was it this dear woman had that so few people seem to have in our time? How might we connect to the source of all life as she did—living so fully, right up to the end of our lives?

These are the questions that sent thousands of people to the Egyptian desert in the 5th century, asking the ammas and abbas there for a "word." They are, I suspect, the questions that drive our contemporary interests in spirituality, self-help, and wholistic well-being. They are the questions that make people like you and me want to read a book like this one.

But here's the trouble: it's hard to find a book today that claims any real authority to address these questions. Yes, we have thousands of books on spirituality. If you've found your way to this one, I imagine you've read several of them.

But this one is different. This is what I most want to say about Enzo Bianchi's fine book. Yes, it's full of wonderful insights. It draws on a great tradition and condenses its wisdom in ways that both surprised and delighted me. It is succinct (which I always appreciate), but also thorough. I could go on.

But what I really want to say is that this is a different kind of spiritual book. It is not the travel journal of a fellow pilgrim, offering thoughts along the way. It's not an enthusiastic promotional for a spiritual practice recently rediscovered. It's not the authoritative tome by the leading scholar in any field.

No, it is different. The best way I know to say it is that reading this book has felt to me like visiting with that dear amma just days before her death. I feel like I'm listening to someone who knows me in my inner most parts. I feel like I'm in the presence of someone who's really alive. And it makes me want to go deeper—to tap into the same living water from which this abba drinks.

This is a book that has made me want to be more holy. It's that simple, really. But I can't imagine anything more important in the whole world.

Jonathan Wilson-Hartgrove
Ordinary Time, 2013

INTRODUCTION

*A*bba, give me a word!" At the beginning of the fourth
century, as Christianity was gradually becoming the
official religion of the Roman Empire and permeating the
customs of the pagan society of the time, this sentence
in its disconcerting simplicity was beginning to resound
more and more frequently in the deserts of Egypt and Palestine,
Syria, and Persia. Passing visitors to monasteries or young
monks often addressed an "elder" in this way, asking for a word
of instruction that, generated by the other's experience of life in
the Spirit, would help them walk in the footsteps of the Lord: *a
word for life* drawn from and thus able to give meaning to everyday
life, a word originating outside of themselves but able to descend
into the heart, an exterior event capable of giving direction to
the listener's inner life. Passed on by word of mouth, welcomed
in the heart of the listener, meditated on, and put into practice,
these words, *echoes of the Word*, soon took the form of a "lexicon of
the desert." By naming the realities of the Spirit, they provided
spirituality with its own vocabulary—and giving a name means
taking a first step toward knowing what one names, toward
acquiring and making one's own an awareness that goes beyond
the name given. Within a short time collections of "sayings and

deeds of the Desert Fathers" appeared, composed to allow these pearls of wisdom to reach a wider audience, to compensate for the inevitable scarcity, with the passing of time, of genuine spiritual "fathers," and to help counter the resulting decline in the quality of Christian life. Those who assembled these anthologies were well aware of their own limitations—in fact, it was this awareness that inspired their desire to communicate messages that would surpass those limitations. They were also aware of the risks their work involved: "The prophets wrote books, the fathers used these books as inspiration for their actions, their successors learned them by heart, our generation copied them on papyrus and parchment and put them away on shelves to gather dust." In one way or another, though, the transmission of ideas took place. Later generations asked questions and found answers, perhaps not directly from an *abba* but from the lines of a manuscript read or copied, or in the context of a community *collatio* or discussion in which ideas were exchanged. In such moments of community dialogue, each person is at the same time *abba* and disciple of the others, on the one condition that he or she speaks and acts with authenticity.

In the following pages, I have sought to make myself an intermediary in this uninterrupted process of transmission. The origin of these pages is similar to the origin of the much more authoritative written anthologies of early Christianity. These pages were written in response to requests from brothers, sisters, and guests of my community, and I have arranged them in book form with the intention of opening this dialogue to a wider but equally interested audience, both within and, more frequently, outside of the church. The most famous early anthologies of sayings were arranged in "alphabetical" order (according to the *abba*'s name) or "systematically" (according to subject), but I have chosen here to use a method of allusions and cross-references in which one term evokes another, explains it in part, and sets aside other elements of the definition to be taken up further on. This method has a long history: it has generated an infinite variety of dictionaries and lexicons, beginning with biblical concordances, and it continues to be the model according to which entries are arranged in modern encyclopedias, even if the order of the entries is strictly alphabetical. It is a method that has found a perhaps unexpected but strikingly current expression in online navigation: what are the celebrated countless Internet "links" if not the fruit of thought associations, of mental connections that have become network connections?

In these pages, then, I have sought to let myself be guided by the biblical and patristic tradition that has preceded and formed me in responding to the requests of those who continue to ask me, with sincerity and passion, for "a reason for my hope" (see 1 Pet. 3:15). In this nonlinear but always directed journey, the reader will at times find him- or herself returning to terrain already traveled, but each time a different perspective is revealed, the point of view changes, a different choice is made at the crossroads. At some "sites" I have paused only briefly, trusting that the topic's richness would emerge with a few key words. At other points—as in the case of prayer, for example—I chose to linger, using different approaches in an attempt to draw as near as possible to the unreachable goal of complete understanding, like a butterfly that dances around a flame but truly understands it only by throwing itself into the fire. This approach is the price I felt it necessary to pay in my efforts to remain open to the guidance of the Spirit, attentive to the newness that makes itself present in our lives, and to the otherness that overturns our carefully made plans. There is a constant that has accompanied me in this journey in Christian spirituality, and it is the conviction that our life has a meaning and that it is not our task to invent it or determine it, but simply to discover it present and active in us and around us. Once we have recognized it, we are given the freedom to welcome it.

ECHOES
of the
WORD

1

SPIRITUAL LIFE

Christian life is impossible without spiritual life! The fundamental responsibility entrusted to the church is that of leading its faithful to an experience of God, a life lived in relationship with God. It is essential today to repeat these basic truths, because we live in a time in which the life of the church, dominated by pastoral concerns, has come to reflect the idea that the experience of faith is based on social involvement rather than on the discovery of a personal relationship with God lived in a community context, rooted in attentive listening to the Word of God contained in Scripture, formed by the Eucharist, and expressed in a life of faith, hope, and love. Reducing the Christian experience to its ethical dimension is the quickest and most direct way to empty faith of its meaning.

Faith leads us to a *genuine experience* of God: in other words, it introduces us to spiritual life, which is life guided by the Holy Spirit. Anyone who believes in God also needs to experience God; correct ideas about God are not enough. The experience of God, which always takes place in a context of faith and not sight (see 2 Cor. 5:7: "We walk by faith, not by sight"), is an experience whose authenticity startles us. We find ourselves repeating with Jacob, "The Lord is in this place—and I did not know it!" (Gen. 28:16), or with the Psalmist, "You hem me in, behind and before. . . . Where can I flee from your presence? If I ascend to heaven, you are there; if I make my bed in Sheol, you are there" (Ps. 139:5, 7–8). At other times our spiritual experience is marked by emptiness, by the silence of God, by an aridity that leads us to repeat Job's words: "If I go forward, he is not there; or backward, I cannot perceive him; on the left he hides, and I cannot behold him; I turn to the right, but I cannot see him" (Job 23:8–9). Yet even in the silence of daily life God can speak to us. He acts in our life through the experiences life offers us, and this means that he also acts in our times of crisis, in the moments of darkness and confusion in which we find ourselves.

The spiritual experience is above all the experience of *being preceded*: it is God who goes before us, searches for us, and calls us. We do not invent the God with whom we want to enter into relationship—he is already there! The experience of God is necessarily mediated by Christ: "No one comes to the Father except through me," says Jesus (John 14:6). The spiritual experience is also the experience of *discovering that we are children of God*. The Holy Spirit is the light with which God lights our path and directs us toward sanctification, and on this path we follow the Son. The spiritual experience becomes nothing other than our response in faith, hope, and love to God the Father, who addresses to each of us, in baptism, the words that reveal our identity: "You are my son," or "You are my daughter." Sons and daughters in Jesus Christ the Son: this is the promise and the path revealed to us in baptism! In the words of Irenaeus of Lyons, the Spirit and the Son are like the two hands with which God shapes our life into a life of freedom in obedience, of relationship and communion with him and with one another.

The authenticity of the spiritual journey depends on several essential elements. The *crisis of our self-image* is the painful but necessary beginning of conversion in which our unreal, idealized "I," the "I" that we have built for ourselves and that we were convinced we needed to develop in our search for self-fulfillment, is shattered. Without this "crisis" we do not arrive at true life according to the Spirit. If we do not die to ourselves we cannot be reborn to the new life offered to us in baptism (see Rom. 6:4). The authenticity of the spiritual journey also depends on honesty toward reality and faithfulness to reality—in other words, adherence to reality—because it is *within* history and *within* daily life, *with* others and not without them, that we come to know God and grow in our relationship with him. It is here that our spiritual life can harmonize obedience to God and faithfulness to the earth in a life of faith, hope, and love. It is here that we can say our "yes" to the God who calls us with the gifts and limitations that characterize our identity as created beings. We are then able to set out on a journey of faith, following in the footsteps of Christ, that will lead us to the experience of Christ dwelling in us. Paul writes to the Christians of Corinth, "Examine yourselves to see whether you are living in the faith. . . . Do you not realize that Jesus Christ is in you?" (2 Cor. 13:5).

The spiritual life unfolds in our "heart," our inmost self, where our desires and decisions take shape. It is here that we should be able to recognize the authenticity of our Christian identity. Our life as Christians is not about going "beyond" or "further," always in search of something new, but rather about going in *depth* and discovering that our heart is the Holy of Holies, the sanctuary of the temple of God that is our body. We discover the meaning of the words "Sanctify the Lord in your hearts" (see 1 Pet. 3:15). It is in our heart that our sanctification—our welcoming the divine life of the Trinity within us—takes place: "Those who love me will keep my word, and my Father will love them, and we will come to them and make our home with them" (John 14:23). The goal of the spiritual life is our participation in the life of God, which the church fathers called "divinization." "God became man so that man could become God," writes Gregory Nazianzen, and in the writings of Maximus the Confessor we find the following sublime summary: "Our divinization takes place when divine love comes to dwell within us, to the point that we forgive our enemies as Christ did on the cross. When is it that you become God? When you are able, like Christ on the cross, to say, 'Father, forgive them,' or even, 'Father, I give my life for them.'" This is the point to which we are led in the spiritual life, a life rooted in faith in God our Father and Creator, set in motion and guided by the Spirit who sanctifies, and lived in communion with the Son who redeems us and teaches us to love as he loved us. It is here that we measure our growth to the full stature of Christ.

2
ASCETICISM

W e are not born Christians, we become Christians" (Tertullian). This "becoming" is the space in which Christian asceticism reveals its meaning. The word *asceticism* is suspect today, if not completely absurd and incomprehensible for many people, including— and this is particularly significant—quite a few Christians. Derived from the Greek verb *askein* (to train or practice), the term *asceticism* indicates a form of methodical training, a repeated exercise, an effort directed toward the acquisition of a specific ability or area of competence. We might think of an athlete, an artist, or a soldier— each trains by repeating over and over the same movements or gestures in order to reach a high level of performance. Asceticism, therefore, is first of all a human necessity, because our growth and "humanization" includes a dimension of interior growth that should correspond to our physical development. We need to know how to say no if we want to be able to say yes: "When I was a child, I spoke like a child, I thought like a child, reasoned like a child; when I became an adult, I put an end to childish ways," writes St. Paul (1 Cor. 13:11). In Christian life, which is rebirth to a new life in Christ and the adaptation of our own life to God's life, we need to learn "unnatural" capacities such as prayer and love for our enemies—and this is impossible without practice and constant effort. Unfortunately, the current cultural myth of spontaneity and permanent adolescence, which sees effort and authenticity as opposed to one another, is a serious obstacle to human maturation and makes it difficult for us to understand why asceticism is essential to spiritual growth.

Of course, it should be said clearly that Christian asceticism always remains *a means directed toward an end*, toward the only goal we can pursue in the spiritual life: *love* for God and our neighbor. It is impossible to practice asceticism without encountering setbacks, failure, and sin, and this helps us realize that Christian asceticism, understood correctly, is always inseparable from grace: "It is not possible to triumph over one's own nature," writes John Climacus. In Christian history there have been numerous exaggerations in ascetic practice, and such excesses have at times threatened to reduce Christian life to a series of heroic feats. At the same time, though, Christians have always spoken out against these excesses, often with a sense of humor: "If you fast regularly, do not be inflated with pride; if you think highly of yourself because of it, then you had better eat meat. It is better for a man to eat meat than to be inflated with pride and glorify himself " (Isidore the Elder). In Christian life, asceticism is not about personal perfection but about growing in freedom and in our relationships with others—the goal is always love. Asceticism takes seriously the fact that we cannot serve two masters, and that the alternative to obeying God is serving idols. We need to "educate" our inner life, refine and purify our love, and continue to make our relationships more intelligent and respectful—this is what asceticism tells us! The "sweat and struggle" (Cabasilas) of our ascetic efforts open us to the gift of God and help us prepare our entire being, our entire existence, to receive the gift of grace. We can summarize the Christian dimension of asceticism in this affirmation: salvation comes from God in Jesus Christ. Asceticism means nothing more than accepting the fact that we are who we are only because of the grace of that Other in our lives named God. It means, in other words, agreeing to receive our identity in our relationship with this Other. Physical asceticism, which has often been viewed in purely negative terms and associated with disdain for the body, especially following the widespread acceptance of a dualistic anthropological model, actually tells us that our experience of God necessarily involves our entire body! Without this dimension, Christianity is reduced either to an intellectual exercise—that is, to gnosis—or to its moral dimension alone.

Asceticism is at the service of the Christian revelation that attests that our true freedom is revealed when we are open to the gift of God and capable of giving ourselves for love of God and our neighbor. Our ascetic discipline has the effect of liberating us from *philautia* ("self-love, egocentrism") and transforming us from individuals into people capable of communion, love, and the free gift of ourselves. Again, the words of a Desert Father reveal that the early Christian tradition recognized its own errors: "Many have prostrated themselves without the slightest discernment, and have left without gaining anything at all. Our mouths smell bad because of our fasting, we know the Scriptures by heart, we recite all of the Psalms, but we do not have what God seeks—love and humility." We need to be intelligent and discerning in our asceticism if we want to please God, and if we want to become more, and not less, human. An intelligent asceticism can help us in our task of making our life a masterpiece, a work of art. Perhaps it is not by chance that the verb *askein*, in ancient Greek literature, is also used to designate the work of the artist. This, then, is the goal of asceticism: to situate the life of the Christian in the domain of beauty, which in Christianity is another name for holiness.

3

HOLINESS AND BEAUTY

The Christian tradition, especially in the West, has interpreted holiness in essentially moral terms. Understood in these terms, holiness does not imply absence of sin, but rather trust in the mercy of God, which is stronger than our sins and able to lift up the believer who has fallen. The holy person is a song sung in thanksgiving for the mercy of God. He or she gives witness to the victory of God three times holy and three times merciful. Holiness is grace; it is a gift, and what is asked of each of us is the fundamental openness that will allow us to be flooded by the divine gift. What holiness tells us above all is that our Christian existence has a responsorial nature—and our response affirms the primacy of who we are over what we do, giving over accomplishing, freedom over legalism. We can say that the nature of Christian holiness, even in its ethical dimension, is not legalistic or juridical, but Eucharistic. It is a response to the *charis* (grace) of God manifested in Jesus Christ, and because of this it is marked by gratitude and joy. The holy person, the saint, is the one who says to God, "Not I, you."

If we think of holiness from the point of view of grace freely offered, we can give it another name: beauty. Yes, in the eyes of the Christian, holiness is also beauty. The New Testament already

makes this association: in the First Letter of Peter, the "holy conduct" to which Christians are called is also described as "beautiful
[or "good"—Greek *kalos*] conduct" (see 1 Pet. 1:15 and 2:12). Seen
as beauty, holiness is no longer an individual effort, the result
of a (perhaps heroic) personal struggle, but an event of communion. It is the communion represented in the iconlike image of
Moses and Elijah "in glory" (Lk. 9:31) and of the disciples Peter,
James, and John gathered around Christ radiant in the light of
the Transfiguration. It is the *communio sanctorum*, the communion of
saints—in other words, the communion of those who participate
in the life of God *communicantes in Unum*, living in communion with
the One who is the only source of holiness (see Heb. 2:11). How
can we forget the cathedral of Chartres, with its statues represent-
ing the holy men and women of the Old and New Testaments
gathered around God like countless rays sent forth by the one
sun? The glory of the One who is "the author of beauty" shines
on the face of Jesus (2 Cor. 4:6), the Messiah celebrated by the
psalmist as "the most beautiful of the sons of men" (Ps. 45:3). This
glory is poured forth into the heart of the Christian by the Holy
Spirit, who transforms our face into the image and likeness of
the face of Christ and our biological individualities into events of
relationship and communion. In this way we as Christians come
to know something of the beauty of the divine life of the Trinity,
a life that is communion, a *perichoresis* of love.

Holiness is the beauty that challenges the ugliness of being
closed in on ourselves, of egocentrism, and of *philautia* (self-love).
It is the joy that challenges the sadness of those who do not open
themselves to the gift of love, like the rich young man of the

Gospel who "went away grieving" (Matt. 19:22). As Léon Bloy has written, "The only sadness is not being holy" (Bloy 1956). This is the holiness, and the beauty, offered to every Christian both as a gift and as a responsibility. In a world called "beautiful" at its creation in the Genesis account (the Hebrew *tor* means both "good" and "beautiful"), men and women are created by God in a relationship of sexual alterity and are made suitable partners for God, capable of receiving the gifts of his love, and this work of creation is praised as "very beautiful" (Gen. 1:31). In a world called to beauty, we who have been given responsibility for creation are also responsible for the beauty of the world, of our own lives, and of each other's lives. If beauty is "a promise of happiness" (Stendhal), every gesture, every word, and every action inspired by beauty is a prophecy of the redeemed world, of the new heavens and new earth, of all humanity reunited in the heavenly Jerusalem in endless communion. Beauty becomes a prophecy of salvation. "It is beauty," Dostoevsky wrote, "that will save the world."

Christians, called to holiness, are also called to beauty, and so we can ask ourselves this question: how have we answered the call to protect beauty, create it, and live in it? There is a beauty that we are called to create in our relationships, a beauty that is capable of making the church a community in which true relationships, based on freedom, mercy, and forgiveness, are possible. In such a community no one can say to another member, "I have no need of you" (1 Cor. 12:21), because every time the communion of the church is damaged, the beauty of the one body of Christ is disfigured. This beauty that we create through our relationships should be capable of making the church a place that is filled with light (see

Matt. 5:14–16), a place of freedom and not of fear, of full expression—and not restriction—of all that is human, of understanding and not opposition, and of sharing and solidarity, especially with the poorest of the poor. It is a beauty that should pervade our living spaces, the liturgy, our physical surroundings, and especially the living temple of God that is each human being. It is the beauty that emerges from simplicity, poverty, and the struggle against idolatry and worldliness. It shines forth where communion triumphs over consumerism, and where contemplation and the free gift of oneself are victorious over possessiveness and greed. Yes, Christianity is *philocalia*, love of beauty, and concealed within the Christian vocation to holiness is a vocation to beauty, an invitation to make our life a work of art, a masterpiece of love. The command "You shall be holy, for I, the Lord, am holy" (Lev. 19:2; 1 Pet. 1:16) is inseparable from the command, "Just as I have loved you, you also should love one another" (John 13:34). Christian beauty is not an object but an event. It is an event of love that narrates again and again in history, creatively and poetically, the folly and tragic beauty of the love with which God has loved us by giving us his Son, Jesus Christ.

4

SENSES AND SPIRIT

The integration of the sensory dimension in the spiritual experience seems problematic today. Does the expression "experience of God" still hold meaning for us? Or must we resign ourselves to letting this experience be diluted to its purely intellectual dimension (speaking or writing about God), reduced to charitable and philanthropic activity (the "experience of God" as altruism), or considered the exclusive privilege of the world of mysticism? We do draw near to God in faith, and not by sight, but we encounter God with our entire self, including our body and senses. Augustine proclaims this: "You called, shouted, broke through my deafness; you flared, blazed, banished my blindness; you lavished your fragrance, I gasped, and now I pant for you; I tasted you, and I hunger and thirst; you touched me, and I burned for your peace" (*Confessions* 10.27.38). Augustine's text echoes the doctrine of the "spiritual senses," first formulated by Origen in the third century. The Alexandrian monk writes:

> Christ becomes the object of each of the soul's senses. He calls himself the true "light" that illuminates the eyes of the soul, the "Word" we hear, the "bread" of life we taste. Similarly, he is called "oil" and "nard" so that the soul can delight in the

fragrance of the Logos, and he became the Word made flesh, tangible and accessible to the touch, so that our inner being can grasp the Word of life. (*Commentary on the Song of Songs* 2.167.25)

In becoming human, God affirmed once and for all the body's eminent spiritual dignity. It is true that the traditional doctrine of the spiritual senses sometimes presupposes a fundamental opposition and division between corporeal and spiritual senses, but in certain versions of the doctrine (in St. Bonaventure, for instance) we perceive the continuity between the two levels of senses. In any case, it is essential that we look beyond the anthropological perspectives, impracticable today, on which the earliest doctrinal formulations were based, and that we retrieve and reformulate the profound spiritual message they were intended to convey. *Sensus fidei*, insight into matters of faith, is grounded not in doctrinal knowledge but in life experience and in a "practical" knowledge of God that allows us to arrive at an "understanding of divine things"—in other words, discernment.

We develop this spiritual discernment above all during the Eucharistic liturgy, where the mystery that is celebrated is the mystery of faith—yet the liturgy is also an experience that involves all of the believer's senses. Those who participate *listen* to the Word of God proclaimed, *see* icons, candles, and the faces of those around them, *taste* the Eucharistic bread and wine, *smell* incense, and *touch* their neighbors as they exchange the sign of peace. The revelation of the Incarnation enters the human person through all of his or her senses, and in the sacramental economy, the celebration of this mystery involves all of the senses, but requires that they be refined and transfigured so that we can perceive all of reality "in Christ." The senses are not eliminated but ordered by faith, trained in prayer, grafted in Christ, and transfigured by the Holy Spirit. The baptized person thus reveals his or her identity as a new creature who truly "'sees' the Son of God, 'hears' and 'listens to' his word, 'touches' him and is nourished by him, 'tastes' him, and breathes life in the Holy Spirit" (Mollat 1974, 231–32). This is how the biblical scholar Donatien Mollat describes the emergence of the spiritual senses in the fourth Gospel. Let us not make the mistake of thinking that this is a "mystical" experience inaccessible to most people. "Listening" to the Word of God during prayerful reading of Scripture leads the believer to "see" the face of Christ and "touch" him in his nearness, "taste" the consolation of the Spirit and shed tears—this is the extreme concreteness of the spiritual experience.

The experience of faith is an experience of beauty, an encounter as real as it is indescribable, an awareness of a presence that is closer to us than our inmost self. And this experience invests the body and the senses. In the Christian East, a holy person is said to have a luminous face and a body that emanates fragrance—his corporeality has become an event of beauty and communion. We should take care, of course, not to confuse the psychological and the emotional with the spiritual, but the spiritual is present in the psychological and invests the body's senses. The "spiritual senses," then, are not simply metaphors, but suggest the different aspects of communion with the Lord that can be revealed to the human mind: gentleness, strength, intimacy, passionate attachment, obedience, the intensity of a presence. This is *sobria ebrietas* (sober drunkenness), the experience of love. When Augustine says that the eye sees "from the heart" and that only love is capable of seeing, he suggests that the spiritual senses are the body's senses permeated by the profound experience of the love of God, a love that purifies, orders, and grants intelligence to human love.

But who today is capable of offering an initiation in "the spiritual life of the body, in a world that, by confusing or separating body and spirit, has lost both and is gradually dying as a result of this loss"? (Cristina Campo 1987).

5

VIGILANCE

A ll we need is a vigilant spirit." This apophthegm of Abba Poemen, a Desert Father, is a strong statement of the centrality of vigilance in Christian spiritual life. In what does it consist? In the New Testament, vigilance is contrasted with drunkenness or drowsiness and defined as the sobriety of those who have a clearly defined goal to pursue and who "keep their eyes open," knowing that if they are not vigilant they may be distracted from their goal. And since the goal to be pursued, for a Christian, is a relationship with God in Jesus Christ, Christian vigilance is completely oriented toward the person of Christ, who has come and who will come again. Basil of Caesarea writes, in the conclusion of his *Moral Rules*, that the Christian's specific identity consists in this vigilance directed toward Christ: "What is it that defines the Christian? Keeping watch every day and hour and being ready to carry out perfectly what pleases God, in the knowledge that the Lord will come at an hour we do not expect." Basil's emphasis on the temporal dimension of vigilance is significant. A type of the vigilant man or woman is the prophet, who translates the gaze and the Word of God into the "today" of time and history. Vigilance is inner lucidity, intelligence, the ability to think critically, awareness of and involvement in the world in which one lives, and freedom from distraction and dissipation. The vigilant person, who has achieved unification by listening to the Word of God and remaining inwardly attentive to the demands of the Word, becomes *responsible*—in other words, radically *not* indifferent, aware of the need to pay attention to his or her surroundings, and in particular, capable of watching over others and taking care of them. "Being an *episcopus* [bishop]," writes Martin Luther, "means looking, being vigilant, keeping careful watch." Vigilance is a quality that demands a great deal of inner strength and, in turn, produces equilibrium: we are asked to be watchful not only with regard to history, the world in which we live, and those around us, but also with regard to ourselves, our own ministry, our work, our personal conduct, and the entire sphere of our relationships. Our vigilance allows Christ to reign as Lord in every aspect of our lives.

This is exactly why vigilance is so difficult: we are asked, first and foremost, to be watchful with regard to ourselves. The Christian's enemy is within, and not outside, him or her. "Be on guard so that your hearts are not weighed down with dissipation and drunkenness and the worries of this life. . . . Be alert at all times and pray," Jesus says in the Gospel of Luke (21:34–36). The price of vigilance is this struggle against ourselves, and those who are vigilant are also resistant. Watchfulness means fighting to defend our inner life, to avoid being distracted by worldly seductions or overcome by life's anxieties, to create unity between our faith and our life, and to maintain balance and harmony in our life. Being vigilant also means adhering to reality instead of using one's imagination as an escape or seeking refuge in idolatry. It means working and avoiding laziness, interacting with others, loving and refusing indifference, and fulfilling one's personal and social commitments in expectation of the coming kingdom of God.

The quality of our life and our relationships depends on our vigilance, which leads us toward fullness of life and helps us fight against the allure of death. Paul tells the Christians of Thessalonica, "Let us not fall asleep as others do, but let us keep awake and be sober" (1 Thess. 5:6). According to biblical symbolism, and in other cultures as well (in Greek mythology, for instance, *Hypnos*, Sleep, and *Thanatos*, Death, are twins), falling asleep means entering the realm of death. Vigilance, on the other hand, is an attitude that characterizes anyone who is attentive and responsible, but it acquires particular significance for the Christian who places his or her faith in Christ, who died and is risen. At the heart of the Christian's vigilance is his or her profound and intimate certainty of the victory of life over death. Those who are vigilant—as opposed to those who are asleep or numb, who dull their inner senses, and who remain on the surface of events and relationships—become fully alert, and they also become men and women of light who are capable of radiating the light that is in them. Christians, "illuminated" through their baptismal immersion, are "children of light" and are called to let their light illuminate others: "Let your light shine before others, so that they may see your good works and give glory to your Father in heaven" (Matt. 5:16). This outpouring of light has nothing to do with spiritual exhibitionism: it happens of its own accord when the light that dwells in a vigilant heart, which cannot remain hidden, overflows and streams forth. In a certain sense, vigilance is the only thing that is absolutely essential in Christian life: it is the source of every virtue, the salt that flavors all of our actions, and the light by which we think and speak. Without vigilance, we run the risk of seeing all of our activity come to nothing. Abba Arsenius said, "Everyone must be watchful of his actions, lest he labor in vain."

6
SPIRITUAL STRUGGLE

The *spiritual struggle* is an essential aspect of Christian spiritual life. The Bible asks believers to prepare themselves to encounter opposition. Just as we are called to "have dominion" within creation, we are also called to dominate ourselves and the sin that threatens us: "Sin is lurking at the door; its desire is for you, but you must master it" (Gen. 4:7). This struggle is an interior one, not directed against those around us but against the temptations, thoughts, suggestions, and inner processes that lead us to consume evil. Paul, using images related to war and athletics (running and boxing), speaks of Christian life as a fight, a sort of inner tension that allows us to remain faithful to Christ, and that involves an unmasking of the processes by which sin gains control over our hearts so that we can fight it at its source. Our heart, in fact, is the site of the battle. In biblical anthropology, the heart is the organ that best represents life in its totality: as the center of the ethical and inner life, the intelligence, and the will, the heart contains all of the elements that constitute what we call the "person" and is similar to how we define "conscience." The Christian spiritual struggle, however, is in no way limited to a psychological process of discernment and adjustment. It is, as Paul tells us, "the fight of faith" (1 Tim. 6:12), the only fight that can be called "good." It is a struggle generated in us by our faith—that is, our bond with Christ revealed in baptism—and undertaken in faith, with trust in the victory Christ himself has already accomplished. It is also a struggle that helps us maintain and strengthen our faith.

In the Christian tradition, the spiritual struggle is intended to protect the believer's "spiritual health." If the goal is *apatheia* (from the Greek *a-pathos*, absence of suffering) this is not intended as *impassibility*, but rather as *absence of pathologies*. This understanding of *apatheia* reveals the therapeutic value of faith at work in the spiritual struggle. Since the spiritual life is a life that is extremely concrete and real, it needs to be nourished and strengthened in order to grow, and it needs to be protected when its integrity is threatened. The Christian traditions of both East and West have identified and described in detail the areas in which Christians struggle spiritually in order to maintain a healthy attitude—in other words, an attitude of communion and not consumerism. In the monastic tradition, it has always been said with force that the life of faith consists in a continuous struggle against temptation. Antony, the "father of monks," said, "The greatest thing a man can do is to throw his faults before the Lord and expect temptation to his last breath." But what is "temptation"?

The word *temptation* designates a thought (the Greek fathers spoke of *logismoi*), suggestion, or stimulus that reaches us either from outside ourselves (what we see or hear, our surroundings) or from within ourselves (from our own psychology, our past, our own personal areas of weakness), and that insinuates in us the possibility of acting in a way that contradicts the gospel. Many of those who attended catechism classes as children remember the list of the "seven deadly sins," widely taught in the Catholic Church from the Counter-Reformation onward but attributable to St. Gregory the Great, who spoke of pride, envy, anger, despair, greed, gluttony, and lust. His list was actually a reformulation of the list of "eight evil thoughts" composed by Evagrius Ponticus in fourth-century Egypt and later published in Latin by John Cassian. If we reread these "sins" today, leaving behind the moralistic and legalistic context in which they have been passed on to us and interpreting them instead as "relationships," they become startlingly relevant (many have seen in them a form of pre-psychoanalysis), and we can grasp the deep and profoundly simple spiritual insight that inspired them.

Evagrius speaks first of *gastrimargia* (gluttony), which concerns not only our relationship with food but any form of eating disorder or imbalance (we might think of anorexia and bulimia). *Porneia* (lust) indicates a lack of balance in our relationship with sexuality, and in particular the tendency to treat our own body or another person's body as an object, to let ourselves be ruled by our impulses, and to reduce to an object of desire a person called to be a subject in a relationship of love. *Philargyria* refers to greed, but on a deeper level it asks us to look closely at our relationships with the objects that surround us, and it challenges our tendency to let ourselves be defined by what we own. *Orge* (anger) can distort our relationships with others to the point of violence, and as Christians we are called to undertake the long and difficult struggle (in other words, the *ascetic* effort) of learning to accept alterity in our relationships. *Lype* indicates sadness or despair, but also the frustration we experience when our relationship with time is out of balance and when we are not able to live in a unified way in the time granted to us. Torn between nostalgia for the past and the desire to escape into an imaginary future, the victim of *spiritus tristitiae* is incapable of living fully in the present. *Akedia* (which does not appear in Gregory the Great's Latinized version of Evagrius's list, probably because it is combined there with *despair*) indicates laziness in the form of *taedium vitae*, a total lack of motivation that in its extreme form can become suicidal. It takes the form of extreme instability, disgust with the way one lives, denial that one's life has meaning, and an inability to live in a harmonic relationship with space. *Kenodoxia* (arrogance, vainglory) is the temptation to define ourselves by what we do, by our work, by what we produce or accomplish. It concerns our relationship with "doing," with action. Finally, *hyperephania* (pride) is hubris in our relationship with God. It is the pride that leads us to exalt our "ego," to substitute our "I" for "God."

These areas, in which every human relationship finds a place, are the "battlefields" of the spiritual struggle. It is not difficult to see that the spiritual struggle seeks to guide the Christian toward personal maturity and the full expression of his or her freedom. Vigilance and attention are the "effort of the heart" (Barsanuphius) that allow the Christian to purify his or her heart. The evil intentions that come from the heart are what defiles, and it is our heart that becomes the dwelling place of Christ through faith. "Guarding the heart" (*phylake tes kardias*) is therefore the spiritual person's task par excellence, the only task that is truly essential. But how is it done? Thanks to the impressive amount of ascetic literature on the subject, from Augustine's *De Agone Christiano* to the writings of Evagrius Ponticus and John Cassian to Lorenzo Scupoli's (1530–1610) well-known treatise *Spiritual Combat*, we can describe in detail the process by which temptation develops in the human heart, a process we need to interrupt and defeat by means of an inner struggle. This process has four fundamental steps or stages: *suggestion, dialogue, consent,* and *passion* (or *vice*). *Suggestion* is the moment in which our heart first considers the possibility of committing a harmful action. We can discern the negative character of the thought from the fact that it generates a certain agitation in our heart, disturbing our peace and serenity. This moment is absolutely universal: no one is exempt from it. If we engage the thought and enter into *dialogue* with it, and if we neutralize (by attempting to justify ourselves) the unease and agitation the thought generates in us, it gradually becomes a presence in our heart that we can no longer dominate and that overcomes us. At this point we *consent*—in other words, we make a personal decision that contradicts the will of God. If we begin to consent repeatedly because we have no ability to struggle, we become enslaved by a *passion* (a vice). This basic process can, however, be interrupted by a struggle that, if we begin it immediately, allows us to destroy these thoughts or suggestions at their source.

Again, what form does this struggle take, in practical terms? Opening one's heart in the context of a relationship with a spiritual mentor is essential, as are prayer and invocation of the Lord, listening to and interiorizing the Word of God, and living a life in which relationships and intense, genuine love are central. The spiritual struggle also requires that we "watch ourselves" and exercise vigilance in all of our relationships, since it is in our relationships that temptation—which we can also call the possibility of idolatry—tries to get a foothold. The forms temptation can take are many, and they reveal themselves in every one of our fundamental relationships: our relationship with food, with our body and our sexuality, with objects (in particular, with money and what we own), with others, with time, with space, with "doing" and working, and with God. Each of these areas of our life, which together define our human and spiritual identity, needs to be ordered and disciplined by means of a spiritual struggle. In all of these areas, temptation tries to seduce us into living with consumerism, instead of communion, as our rule. This is why the Eucharist, which celebrates life lived in communion with God and those around us, teaches us a great deal about struggling against temptation.

In the spiritual struggle we need patience and persistence. We need to know, first of all, how to discern the tendencies that lead us in the direction of sin, and we need to be able to identify our own areas of personal fragility and weakness and what is negative in us. We then need to name these things and accept responsibility for them, rather than ignoring or repressing them. Finally, we can begin the long and difficult struggle that will allow the Word and the will of God to reign in us! The heart—intended biblically as the organ responsible more for our will and our decisions than for our feelings—is the site of the struggle. If we want to welcome the Word of God in our heart, the ability to struggle spiritually, to learn "the art of battle" (see Pss. 18:35; 144:1) is essential. Without it, "the cares of the world, and the lure of wealth, and the desire for other things come in and choke the word" in our heart, and it "yields nothing" (Mk. 4:19). Those with experience in the spiritual life know that this combat is more difficult than any external struggle, but they also come to know the fruit of peace, freedom, gentleness, and love it produces. It is through the experience of struggle that faith becomes faith that remains, perseverance. And it is through struggle that our love is ordered and purified. Athenagoras, ecumenical patriarch of Constantinople, said:

> If we want to fight evil effectively, we have to fight within ourselves and defeat the evil that is in us. It is a bitter war, this war against ourselves. I fought it for years and years, and it was terrible. But now I am disarmed. I am no longer afraid of anything, because "love drives out fear." I have been disarmed of the desire to get the better of others, to justify myself at the expense of someone else. No, I am no longer afraid. When we no longer possess anything, we have no fear. "Who will separate us from the love of Christ?" (Clément 1969, 183)

Indeed, temptation, wrote Origen, "turns the Christian into a martyr or an idolater."

Spiritual listlessness": this is how the fourth-century Egyptian monk Evagrius Ponticus describes *akedia*, the spiritual malaise whose name has virtually no equivalent in a modern language and whose nuances include disgust with life, boredom, discouragement, laziness, sleepiness, melancholy, nausea, sadness, and lack of enthusiasm and motivation. John Cassian (fourth–fifth century) transliterated the Greek *akedia* into Latin as *acedia*, and about a century later St. Gregory the Great identified *acedia* with *tristitia* in his list of the capital sins. *Akedia*, which according to Evagrius afflicts anchorites in particular (those who live a monastic life that emphasizes solitude), has only been closely observed and analyzed in monastic environments, but it is "a phenomenon common to all humanity; in fact, it is the price of being human," writes Father Gabriel Bunge (1969, 91), an eminent scholar of Evagrius.

Akedia manifests itself as an instability that makes the subject incapable of maintaining a balanced relationship with space and time. Monastics who suffer from *akedia* find the effort of remaining in the solitude of their cell unbearable, are unable to inhabit their own body (*habitare secum*), and have the impression that time passes unbearably slowly. Evagrius writes, "*Akedia* makes the sun appear to be slow-moving or even motionless, and the day seems to last fifty hours." *Akedia* is a sort of asphyxiation or suffocation of the spirit that condemns those who suffer from it to unhappiness by causing them to reject what they have or the situation (work-related, emotional, or social) in which they live, and to dream about another situation that is unattainable. Those who find themselves in this condition easily fall prey to various fears (for instance, the fear of illnesses more imaginary than real) and become inefficient in their work, intolerant, impatient with others (who often become the target of the affected person's frustration and aggression), and incapable of controlling the thoughts that flood their minds and cast them into profound discouragement and dissatisfaction with themselves, causing them to wonder whether perhaps everything they have done in their lives has been a mistake. *Akedia* can, in fact, become a depressive condition (the *Catechism of the Catholic Church* [1992] calls it "a form of depression due to the slackening of asceticism, lack of vigilance, and failure to guard the heart") in which subjects are tempted to break with their past—for example, by abandoning their marriage or religious vows, or by making another "change"—or even to consider suicide. *Akedia*, writes Isaac the Syrian, "gives a taste of hell."

In early monastic descriptions, *akedia* is the "midday demon" that strikes most often during the hours when the desert heat is most oppressive (between ten in the morning and two in the afternoon), before the single meal monks shared around three in the afternoon. In the writings of Pascal, Baudelaire, Kierkegaard, Guardini, Bergson, and Jankélévitch, we find observations that are analogous, at least in part, to these early monastic descriptions of *akedia*, and others have noted similarities to forms of depression described in psychology. It is especially interesting to consider the analogy that has been drawn between the phenomenon of *akedia*, which tends to strike at midday, and the midlife crisis, which usually strikes between the ages of thirty-five and forty. "There seems to be a biological basis for the sense of apprehension, the tormented questions, and the lack of enthusiasm men and women experience in their late thirties. Could this be the state of mind medieval scholars called *accidia*, the capital sin of spiritual laziness? I think it is" (Church 1993, 20). Those who undergo a midlife crisis and those who suffer from *akedia* experience many of the same reactions: denial, repression, self-deprecation, obsession with power, legalistic rigidity, depression, a tendency to eat and drink excessively, and numbness, among others.

How can we combat *akedia*? First, by accepting the limits that define human existence, namely, the passing of time and mortality (the monastic fathers recommended practicing *memoria mortis*), by taking responsibility for our past, and by accepting our own limitations and imperfections. Perseverance, patience (which is the art of living with what is incomplete), prayer, living a life in which relationships are central, involving one's body in work that is physically demanding, and seeking help (the monastic fathers advised seeking a "spiritual father" or guide) are other important elements of the struggle. Evagrius offers the following words of advice: "Set a measure for yourself in everything you do." In other words, organize your time, set a schedule for yourself, and take responsibility for your life.

8
DESERT

F or me the experience of the desert has been dominant. Between sky and sand, between Everything and Nothing, the question burns. Like the burning bush, it burns without being consumed. It burns for itself, in the emptiness. The desert is also the experience of listening, the extreme of listening" (Jabès 1978, 56). Perhaps it is this connection with listening that makes the desert a "presence" always rich in spiritual significance, so important in the Bible. The desert, of course, is first and foremost a place, and it is a place that has different names in biblical Hebrew: there is the *caravah*, the arid and uncultivated stretch of land that extends from the Dead Sea to the Gulf of Aqaba; the *khorbah*, which has a psychological rather than strictly geographical connotation and indicates a desolate wasteland, inhabited by forgotten ruins; the *yeshimon*, a solitary wilderness without roads or water; and most importantly, the *midbar*, a vast, flat, inhospitable expanse inhabited by wild animals, where the only plants are shrubs and thorn bushes. The biblical desert is almost never a desert of sand. It is a product of the erosion caused by wind and rare but violent rainstorms, and it is characterized by sharp fluctuations in temperature between day and night (see Ps. 121:6).

Resistant to the presence of human beings and hostile toward life (Num. 20:5), the desert, a place of death, represents in the Bible the necessary education of the believer, the process of initiation during which the group of slaves who leave Egypt become the people of God. In essence, it is a place of rebirth. Wasn't the world born as an ordered cosmos out of the chaos, the formless wasteland that existed before creation? In Genesis the earth, marked by absence and negativity ("In the day that the LORD God made the earth and the heavens . . . no plant of the field was yet in the earth and no herb of the field had yet sprung up—for the LORD God had not caused it to rain upon the earth," Gen. 2:4–5), becomes, through creation, the garden prepared for humanity (Gen. 2:8–15). And isn't the new creation, the messianic era, described as a time when the desert will burst into bloom? "The wilderness and the dry land shall be glad; the desert shall rejoice and blossom; like the crocus it shall blossom abundantly" (Isa. 35:1–2). But between the first creation and the new creation stretches the *creatio continua*, God's saving work in history. It is during this expanse of history that the desert becomes the site of God's great revelations: in the *midbar* ("desert"), says the Talmud, God reveals himself as *medabber*, the one who speaks. In the desert Moses sees the burning bush and receives the revelation of the Name (Exod. 3:1–14); in the desert God gives his people the law, meets with them and binds himself in a covenant with them (Exod. 19–24); in the desert he offers his people gifts in abundance (manna, quail, water from the rock); in the desert he reveals his presence to Elijah in "a sound of sheer silence" (1 Kgs. 19:12); in the desert he draws Israel, his bride, back to him after her betrayal (Hos. 2:16), and renews his marriage covenant with his people.

This gives us an idea of the fundamental semantic bipolarity, negative-positive, of the desert in the Bible, which embraces the three general symbolic areas to which the desert refers us: space, time, and the journey. The hostile space of the desert must be crossed before we can reach the Promised Land. Time, in the desert, is long but has an end—it is an "intermediate" time of waiting, hope, and longing. There is a long and difficult journey, beginning with a departure from slavery and ending with an arrival in a land that is welcoming, a land of "milk and honey": this is the desert of the exodus! The spaciousness of the desert—arid, monotonous, silent—reverberates in the believer's inner landscape as trial and temptation. Was the exodus worth it? Wouldn't it have been better to stay in Egypt? What kind of salvation is this if we are hungry and thirsty, and if every day offers us the sight of the same horizon? It is not easy to accept the fact that the desert is an integral part of salvation! Israel puts God to the test in the desert, whose vast emptiness turns out to be a terrible scrutiny, a revelation of what inhabits the human heart. "Remember the long way that the LORD your God has led you these forty years in the wilderness, in order to humble you, testing you to know what was in your heart, whether or not you would keep his commandments" (Deut. 8:2). The desert is an education in self-knowledge, and perhaps the journey undertaken by Abraham, the father of believers, in response to God's invitation, "Go forth"! (Gen. 12:1; the Hebrew can also be translated, "Go toward yourself") captures the spiritual significance of the journey through the desert. The desert is the site of rebellion against God, complaints, and grumbling (Exod. 14:11–12; 15:24; 16:2–3, 20–27; 17:2–3, 7; Num. 12:1–2; 14:2–4; 16:3–4; 20:2–5;

21:4–5). Jesus also experiences the desert as a necessary form of novitiate or preparation for his ministry: his face-to-face encounter with the power of satanic illusion and the attraction of temptation reveals that his heart is attached to the Word of God alone (Matt. 4:1–11). Strengthened by his struggle in the desert, Jesus can begin his public ministry.

The desert also appears in the Bible as an "intermediate" time, a "time between": one can travel through the desert but not settle there. Forty years, forty days: this is the "time of the desert" for the people of Israel during their journey, but also for Moses, Elijah, and Jesus. It is a stretch of time that can be endured only if we learn to be patient, to wait and to persevere, accepting the high price of hope. Perhaps the immensity of time in the desert is already an experience and foretaste of eternity! But the desert is also a journey. We must continue to go forward without "deserting," despite the temptation to regress and the fear that pushes us to turn back and choose the security of slavery in Egypt over the risk of the adventure of freedom—and this freedom is to be found not at the end of the journey, but during the journey. In order to set out, we need to travel lightly—the desert teaches us to recognize what is essential and is an apprenticeship in reduction and simplification. It also educates us in faith by sharpening our inner vision, giving us an eye that penetrates, and making us vigilant. A man or woman of the desert is able to recognize the presence of God and denounce idolatry. In John the Baptist, man of the desert par excellence, everything is reduced to the essential—in him we find a "voice that cries out" and calls for conversion, a hand that points toward the Messiah, an eye that searches deeply and discerns sin, a body carved by the desert, an existence transformed into a journey toward the Lord ("In the wilderness prepare the way of the Lord!," Isa. 40:3). His food is frugal, his clothing reveals that he is a prophet, and he himself decreases in front of the one who comes after him. He has learned well the desert's economy of diminution. But he has also experienced the desert as a meeting place, a place of friendship and love: he is the friend of the bridegroom who stands next to the bridegroom and rejoices at the sound of his voice.

The biblical desert leaves us with this ambivalence. We can see it as a figure of the ambivalence of human life, of the believer's daily experience, and of the contradictory experience of God himself. Perhaps Henri Le Saux was right in saying, "God is not in the desert. It is the desert itself that is the mystery of God" (Le Saux 1979, 158).

9

WAITING FOR THE LORD

s we eat this bread and drink this cup, we
proclaim your death, Lord Jesus Christ, until you come
in glory." These words at the heart of the Eucharistic
celebration remind Christians of a central aspect of
their identity and life of faith: waiting for the coming
of the Lord. "The Christian," wrote Cardinal Newman,
"is one who waits for Christ." Of course, in a society that wants
to have everything immediately, that values speed and productivity, and in which even Christians can often be identified by their
frenetic activity, anyone who talks about waiting is not likely to
be popular and may very well encounter total incomprehension.
For many, waiting is a synonym for passivity, inertia, and the evasion of responsibility. But Christians, who do not let themselves
be defined simply by what they do but by their relationship with
Christ, know that the Christ they love and in whom they place
their trust is the Christ who has come, who comes today, and
who will come in glory. They have before them not nothingness
or emptiness but a hope that is certain, an expectation, a future
whose meaning is centered on the Lord's promise, "Surely, I am
coming soon" (Rev. 22:20). The verb "to wait," from the Latin
ad-tendere, suggests a "stretching toward," an "attention directed
toward," a motion of the spirit in the direction of an Other, a

future. We can even call waiting an action—not an action contained within the present, but one that will bring about a future outcome. The Second Letter of Peter expresses this dimension of waiting when it tells us that Christians hasten, through their expectation, the coming of the day of the Lord (2 Pet. 3:12).

This specifically Christian view of time makes the believer one who has hope (see 1 Thess. 4:13), who waits for Christ (Phil. 3:20; Heb. 9:28), and who is defined not only by his or her past but also by the future and what will be accomplished by Christ in that future. Such a view of time can be a valuable form of testimony (or perhaps countertestimony) in a world in which time is often seen as empty, as evolving in a continuum that excludes any kind of active waiting and that generates the fatalism and inability to wait typical of our modern mentality. If Christians fail to understand and live up to the Christian understanding of time, they deprive faith of its full meaning, and they also deprive the world of a profession of hope it has the right to receive from Christians (see 1 Pet. 3:15).

As human beings we *are* expectation. If this basic anthropological dimension of waiting, which reminds us that we ourselves are "unfinished," is not recognized, we come face-to-face with the risk of idolatry—which always means seeing the present moment as sufficient in itself. The expectation of the Lord's coming, on the other hand, requires Christians to *wait* for what is about to come and to wait with patience for what will come at a moment they do not expect. Patience is the art of living within the incompleteness and fragmentary nature of the present moment without giving in to despair. It is the ability to respect time, to live within its limits and to persevere, to respect others in their weaknesses and limitations, and to carry them. Our expectation of and ardent desire for the Lord's coming make us men and women capable of patience, with regard to time and in our relationships with each other.

It is in this context that we discover that patient waiting is a sign of strength, firmness, stability, and conviction, not weakness. Patience is above all the attitude that reveals a deep love for God and for others: "Love is patient" (1 Cor. 13:4). When our waiting is inspired by love, it becomes desire, desire to be with our Lord (2 Cor. 5:2; Phil. 1:23). As we wait for the Lord, we learn to desire and to discipline our desire, to keep a distance between ourselves and the things we desire, and to transform our consumeristic attitude into an attitude of sharing and communion, an attitude that is Eucharistic. Waiting for the Lord generates gratitude and thanksgiving in us, and it allows us to open our heart outward, to unite it to the longing of all of creation: "The creation waits with eager longing for the revealing of the children of God" and hopes to be "set free from the bondage to decay" (Rom. 8:19–21). The entire creation is waiting for new heavens and a new earth, transfiguration, the kingdom of God. As Christians await the Lord's coming, their expectation becomes an invocation of universal salvation, an expression of a faith that embraces the entire cosmos and suffers together with every human being and every creature. If this is what it means to wait for the Lord, and if this waiting is a responsibility we have as Christians, we should listen to Teilhard de Chardin's heartfelt and provocative message: "We Christians, responsible, after Israel, for keeping the ardent flame of desire burning—what has become of our longing?" (de Chardin 1957, 197).

10
PATIENCE

The Bible attests that patience is above all a divine prerogative: according to Exodus 34:6 God is *makrothymos*, "forbearing," "long-suffering," "patient." (The equivalent expression in Hebrew has the literal meaning of "slow to anger.") The God who entered into a covenant with a "stiff-necked" people cannot be other than patient! The full extent of God's patience was manifested in his sending his Son Jesus Christ and in Christ's death for sinners, and this patience is still what sustains the present: "The Lord is not slow about his promise . . . but is patient [*makrothymei*] with you, not wanting any to perish, but all to come to repentance" (2 Pet. 3:9). God's patience in the Bible is expressed through the fact that he is the God who speaks: by speaking, he gives the listener time to respond, and waits for him or her to make a change of heart. The patience of God should not be confused with impassibility: on the contrary, it is the "endurance of his passion" (Jüngel 1985, 11) and the far-reaching gaze of his love, a love that "has no pleasure in the death of sinners, but that they turn from their ways and live" (see Ezek. 33:11). It is a force that is active even when we have not yet set out on the path of conversion. The patience of God finds its most eloquent expression in the passion and cross of Christ: here the dissymmetry between God, who waits patiently, and sinful humanity increases beyond measure in the passionate love and suffering of God in his crucified Son Jesus Christ. Since the moment of the death of Christ on the cross, patience as a Christian virtue has been a gift of the Spirit (Gal. 5:22) granted by the crucified and risen Christ, and a participation in the energies that have their origin in the Paschal event.

For Christians, patience is inseparable from faith, and it includes both perseverance—faith that endures with the passing of time—and *makrothymia*, the art of "taking a step back" in order to see the entire picture, and of accepting the incompleteness of the present. This second aspect tells us that patience is necessarily humble. As we discover that we ourselves are incomplete, we learn to be patient with ourselves; as we recognize the incompleteness and fragility of our relationships with others, we learn to be patient with those around us; and as we confess that the divine plan of salvation has not yet been fully accomplished, we express our patience through our hope, our invocation, and our longing for salvation. Patience is the virtue of a church that waits for the Lord, living responsibly within the "not yet" of salvation without trying to anticipate an end not yet revealed and without proclaiming itself as the fulfillment of God's design. Patience refuses the impatience of certain mysticisms and ideologies and chooses the "long route" of listening, obeying, and waiting for others and for God. It seeks to build the communion that can be built within the limits of time and history. Patience is respect for the time another person needs and awareness of the fact that we experience time together, "in the plural," and that it is our shared experience of time that makes relationships, communication, and love possible. Given the fascination today with the idea of "time without constraints"—according to which freedom is often imagined as an absence of commitments and restrictions, or as the possibility to go back to an uncontaminated point of departure and begin again from one day to the next, erasing or repressing all of one's past experiences, and especially one's relationships and commitments—it may seem irrelevant or inappropriate to speak about patience, but the subject urgently needs to be addressed. For Christians, patience is as central as agape, as Christ himself. The ability to be patient—that is, to accept the time of the other (God or another person) as something that defines our own existence—is the work of love. "Love is patient" (*makrothymei*), writes Paul (1 Cor. 13:4). The Christian's patience is genuine and lasting only to the extent that it is rooted in "the patience of Christ" (*hypomone tou Christou*, 2 Thess. 3:5).

It is not difficult to see why the church fathers often spoke of patience as the *summa virtus*, the greatest virtue (see Tertullian, *De patientia* 1.7): it is an essential element of faith, hope, and love. Cyprian of Carthage writes, "It is faith and hope that make us Christians, but if faith and hope are to produce fruit, they require patience" (Cyprian, *De bono patientiae* 13). Patience, together with faith in Christ, becomes perseverance and "the strength to face ourselves" (Thomas Aquinas). It allows us to resist discouragement and despair in times of trial, to hold out in a given situation over a long period of time without letting the truth of who we are become distorted, and to endure and sustain others and their situations. There is nothing heroic about this spiritual endeavor: all we need is the faith that we in turn are held up by the outstretched arms of Christ on the cross.

Christians are sustained in the difficult task of patience by a promise: "The one who endures to the end will be saved" (Matt. 10:22; 24:13). Enduring means remaining firm in a profession of faith, but it also means expressing our patience actively, supporting others in our ecclesial and community relationships ("bear with one another," Col. 3:13), as well as in our relationships *ad extra*, with those outside the Christian community ("be patient with all," 1 Thess. 5:14). When we express our patience in this way, it becomes an aspect of our faith that provokes a continual reassessment of the internal structure of the Christian community, the community's understanding of its place in the world, and the way it situates itself among people of other beliefs. Christian patience challenges the status quo, and as it provokes, it also disquiets!

11

FAITHFULNESS AND TIME

O that today you would listen to his voice!" (Ps. 95:7): in the Bible, it is Israel's covenant with God that gives time its meaning. The "existential" time in which the people of God lives is granted to them through the *davar* (word-event) of the Lord and through their own obedience to this word. In the Bible, time is always tied to the radically historical nature of human existence, and to the fact that each of us is created by God with the capacity to choose *today* between life and death, the blessing and the curse. History itself is directed toward a *telos* (goal) revealed through the actions of God, who manifests himself in humanity's progress and regressions. Our history is a story of salvation because God continues to call humanity to walk toward the light, toward the goal of the kingdom, and because he continues to inspire in us the longing for shalom, which is both God's gift and the highest achievement of human faithfulness.

We find this biblical understanding of time developed further in the New Testament: in the "fullness of time" (Gal. 4:4) God sends his Son, born of a woman, and the life and passion-death-resurrection of Jesus are single historical events that take place in a specific moment of history and mark the beginning of the "last days," a time in which we await Jesus's return in glory, the coming of the kingdom, and the renewal of the entire cosmos. With the first coming of Jesus we witness the beginning of a *kairos*, a "time of favor" that defines all of time from that moment onward. "The time is fulfilled" (Mk. 1:15), Jesus announces as he begins his ministry: it is time to repent and believe in the gospel (Mk. 1:15; Matt. 4:17), because the time of fulfillment has begun. This means that we are asked to use time well: the time of favor is a reality in Jesus Christ! The passion, death, and resurrection of Jesus are not simply past events; they are the reality of the present, and our concrete today is flooded in the light of salvation. Now is the acceptable time, now is the day of salvation (see 2 Cor. 6:2)!

The Christian's first attitude with regard to time, then, is that of recognizing in his or her own "today" the "today" of God. As we listen to and obey the Word that resounds *today*, our relationship with time—in Greek mythology, the tyrant Chronos who devours his children—is transformed and takes on specific characteristics: we discover that we need to interpret the present time (see Lk. 12:56) and "interpret the signs of the times" (Matt. 16:3) in order to recognize the time of our visitation by God (Lk. 19:44). We know that our time is in God's hands: "I say, 'You are my God.' My times are in your hand" (Ps. 31:14–15). This is our fundamental attitude: our days do not belong to us; they are not our property. Time belongs to God, and for this reason the psalmist says to God, "Lord, let me know my end, and what is the measure of my days" (Ps. 39:4), and asks, "Teach us to count our days that we may gain a wise heart" (Ps. 90:12). Our wisdom consists in knowing how to count our days and recognize them as a time of favor, as God's today that breaks into our own today.

Christians are asked to "be alert at all times and pray" (Lk. 21:36) because they are involved in a struggle against idolatry in which the idol, the tyrant who seeks to dominate and enslave, is alienated time. According to Paul, Christians should try to take full advantage of the time they have available, and use it for doing good (see Gal. 6:10). They are called, above all, to use their wisdom to save, set free, and redeem time (see Eph. 5:16; Col. 4:5).

All of this derives from the Christian experience of time as struggle, trial, and suffering. Even after the victory of Christ and the communication of the energies of the resurrection to Christians, the influence of the "god of this age" (2 Cor. 4:4) is still present in the world, and time remains a time of exile and pilgrimage (see 1 Pet. 1:17) in which Christians await the eschatological reality in which God will be all in all (see 1 Cor. 15:28). Today, in a time in which many tend to limit their attention to what is current and immediate and no longer have the courage to speak about perseverance, let alone eternity, Christians know—and repeat tirelessly—that time opens into eternity and eternal life, into a time filled by God alone. This is the goal toward which all time is directed, and in it "Jesus Christ is the same yesterday, and today, and forever" (Heb. 13:8; cf. Rev. 1:18). The telos of our lives is eternal life, and our days are an expression of our longing for the coming of God. If this is the authentic dimension of time for the Christian, we can understand the full weight of these words of Dietrich Bonhoeffer: "Is not the loss of our moral memory the reason behind the dissolving of all personal ties— love, marriage, friendship, faithfulness? Nothing lasts, nothing takes root. Everything is short-term, everything is temporary. But great things such as justice, truth, beauty and in general all great accomplishments demand time, stability, and 'memory,' or they degenerate. Someone who is not willing to bear responsibility for a past and give form to a future is someone who is 'memoryless,' and I do not know how such a person can be confronted, shaken, or made to reflect" (Bonhoeffer 1973, 215).

Written more than fifty years ago, these words are still very relevant in the way they address the issues of faithfulness and perseverance. These realities are rare today, and often we no longer know how to define the words themselves—at times, they are even felt to be suspect or dated, and we abandon all hope for their return to those who are nostalgic for "old-fashioned values." But if faithfulness is an essential virtue in any interpersonal relationship, perseverance is the virtue that is specifically related to time, and in our relationships we are confronted with the demands of both. In addition to this, the values that we all proclaim fundamental and absolute depend on faithfulness and perseverance. How can there be justice if those who are just are not also faithful? How can there be freedom without the perseverance of those who are free? Without faithfulness and perseverance, no other value or virtue exists! Without faithfulness, for that matter, we are unable to build anything together with others. Today, our experience of time as fragmented and devoid of restrictions and boundaries makes faithfulness and perseverance a necessary challenge for all, and for Christians in particular. Christians know that their God is faithful and has made his faithfulness known in his Son Jesus Christ, "the Amen, the faithful and true witness" (Rev. 3:14) in whom "every one of God's promises is a Yes" (2 Cor. 1:20).

Perseverance and faithfulness, then, are tied to the historical, temporal, relational, incarnate nature of Christian faith, and they define faith as a responsibility to be assumed within the limits of our historical existence. Faith becomes something other than an abstraction only when it defines and shapes the entire span of our existence, until our death. Christians know that their faithfulness is sustained by God's faithfulness to his covenant, expressed in the history of salvation as faithfulness toward those who are unfaithful and as forgiveness. In taking upon himself, through the Incarnation and Paschal event, our human situation of sin, poverty, and death, God has expressed his faithfulness as total and unlimited responsibility for humanity and for each person. This means that the values of faithfulness and perseverance lead us directly to the even more radical issue of responsibility. Those who are irresponsible, like those who are narcissistic, will never be faithful. This is also true because genuine faithfulness is always faithfulness to a "you"—either a person we love or a cause we love almost as we would a person—and this means that not every form of faithfulness is authentic! Holding a grudge against someone is, in a way, a form of faithfulness, but it is a form of faithfulness governed by hatred. The faithfulness we are speaking about here is an expression of *love*, is accompanied by *gratitude*, and includes the *ability to stand firm* in times of difficulty and contradiction.

Jankélévitch defines faithfulness as "the determination to not give in to the temptation of apostasy" (Jankélévitch 1970, 413).

Faithfulness is an active struggle whose arena is the human heart, and it is only possible when one's heart is committed! This means that our faithfulness depends on our inner freedom, our human maturity, and our love. The situations of infidelity we encounter in our daily lives, situations in which a commitment or relationship is abandoned, often point to a problem in one of these areas. This is why we cannot, in the church, reduce the problem of faithfulness and perseverance, and their opposites, to a strictly juridical dimension, considering them solely from the point of view of laws to be observed. There is always the mystery of a person in question, and not simply an act of separation to be sanctioned. The act of separation should be considered revelatory of the situation of the heart—in other words, the inner identity—of the person in question. We should also remember that the dimension of infidelity is present within our faithfulness itself, just as doubt is present in the believer's heart. What is the Bible other than the testimony of the people of Israel's stubborn faithfulness in telling the story of their own infidelity in response to the faithfulness of God? How can we recognize our own faithfulness unless we see it as faith in the One who is faithful? In this sense, a "faithful" Christian is a Christian who is capable of *memoria Dei*, who remembers the actions of the Lord: by constantly remembering God's faithfulness, we are sustained in our own faithfulness at the very moment in which our infidelity is revealed to us. This is exactly what happens at the heart of the life of the church, during the Eucharistic anamnesis.

12
CONVERSION

epent, and believe in the good news!" (Mk. 1:15). "Repent, for the kingdom of heaven has come near!" (Matt. 4:17). A call for conversion is at the heart of the two different versions of the exclamation that marks the beginning of Jesus's preaching ministry. Following in the footsteps of Hosea, Jeremiah, and all the prophets up to John the Baptist who called for a *return to the Lord* (see Matt. 3:2), Jesus asks for conversion, or return (*teshuvah* in Hebrew), to the one true God. Conversion is also the theme of the early church's preaching and the preaching of the apostles (see Acts 2:38; 3:19), and it is the church's essential message and responsibility in every age. The root of the Hebrew verb *shuv*, "to return," can also mean "to answer," which tells us that conversion, the act of returning again and again to the Lord, is the responsibility of the entire church and of each individual Christian. Conversion is not an ethical demand, and although it does imply distancing oneself from idols and sin (see 1 Thess. 1:9; 1 Jn. 5:21), its motivation and foundation is eschatological and Christological. It is in relation to the gospel of Jesus Christ and the kingdom of God, close at hand in Christ, that the reality of conversion takes on its full meaning. Only a church in which faith is central can understand conversion as a dimension of daily life, and it is only when the church makes conversion a reality in its own life that it can claim the role of credible witness to the gospel in history and among humanity, and thus evangelize. Only women and men changed by the gospel, who demonstrate their conversion to others through the way they live, are able to request conversion of others. Without personal conversion, we do not announce salvation and are completely incapable of asking others to make a change. Christians whose lives remain focused on worldly concerns can do no more than encourage others to remain as they are: by preventing others from seeing the effectiveness of salvation, they impede evangelization and weaken the gospel's force. In one of John Chrysostom's homilies, we read: "You can't preach? You can't spread the word of doctrine? In that case, teach with your actions and your behavior, O newly baptized. When those who saw you immodest or sinful, corrupt or indifferent, see you changed and converted, you can be sure they will say, as the Jews said to the man blind from birth who was healed, 'Is it him?' 'It is!' 'No, he looks just like him.' 'Isn't it him?'"

We can say, in summary, that conversion is not only the initial moment of faith in which we arrive at belief in God by leaving behind a previous situation; it is the *form faith takes in our lives*. A problem arises here for most Christians: those whose familial environment is Christian and who are baptized at birth, receive religious instruction, and are introduced to ecclesial life as part of their upbringing do not normally experience a change between a *before* and an *after*, between a non-Christian situation and the journey toward faith that characterizes the Christian "convert." On the other hand, we are once again seeing people today who return to Christian life after many years spent "in exile" from faith, or who call themselves converted because they have met Christ in an unexpected way—or perhaps because they have reached, over time, the point of making a full commitment to Christianity. The phenomenon of conversion is thus reappearing, even in countries where Christianity has been present for centuries. This can help all Christians understand that conversion truly is essential, and that Christian life itself can only be understood in terms of continually renewed conversion. Conversion attests that Christianity is perennially young: a Christian is one who continues to say, "Today I am beginning again." Its source is faith in the resurrection of Christ. No fall, no sin has the last word in Christian life, and our faith in the resurrection makes us able to believe more strongly in God's mercy than in the evidence of our own weakness, and to set out again on the path of faith, following Christ. Gregory of Nyssa writes that in Christian life we go forward "from beginning to beginning, across beginnings that never end." Yes, conversion is always essential for the church and for each Christian, because we are always called to recognize the idols that appear in our midst and to renew our struggle against them, in order to show that it is God who is Lord of our lives and of reality. When the entire church makes conversion a part of its life, it recognizes that God is the Lord, not the church's possession. Conversion implies the expression in the church's life of the eschatological dimension of faith—in other words, the longing for the coming kingdom of God that the church does not possess but announces through the testimony of its own conversion.

13
ATTENTION

The Christian tradition has defined *prosoche*, "attention," as an attitude of "concentration," an inner "stretching toward," a "focusing of the mind." The Greek word has a dynamic connotation, as do the Latin *attentio* and *attendere*, which tells us that someone who is attentive is someone who "reaches" toward something. Attention is not the activity of a particular human faculty as much as a movement of the entire person, body and spirit. Once we have discovered the meaning, center, and goal of our existence, attention becomes the unification of our actions in the light of that goal, our profound dedication to that center. Growing in attention means growing in personal unification. Asian forms of ascetic discipline and meditation are profoundly familiar with attention: in Buddhism, it is through attention that one reaches a penetrating vision of reality, a way of seeing, what the Desert Fathers and the Christian tradition have called *diorasis* (seeing in depth, beyond appearances and exteriors). In Christianity, *prosoche* derives from the Jewish teaching called *kawwanah*, which indicates inner attention and vigilance of the heart and senses in one's relationship with God, attachment of one's entire being to the words of prayer and Scripture, and most importantly, attachment to the presence of God reached through these words.

This is why attention, in the Christian tradition, is requested in particular during the celebration of the liturgy (*opus Dei*) and during personal reading of the Bible (*lectio divina*).

But attention is a reality whose meaning is infinitely deeper. It is a lucid "presence to oneself" that becomes discernment of the presence of God in the human person. Basil, commenting on the Bible verse "Be careful" (Deut. 15:9), writes, "Pay attention to yourself if you want to pay attention to God." This attention to ourselves means resisting the thoughts that distract us by drawing us away from our center, and it becomes a way of guarding the heart: "Attention is the silence of the heart uninterrupted by thoughts" (Hesychius of Batos). There is an aspect of struggle inherent in attention that involves keeping watch over the thoughts that appear in the heart, recognizing their nature and origin, destroying those that are harmful, and resisting the suggestion of a harmful thought before it becomes dialogue (inner conversation with the thought) and results in action, or consumption of sin. Through this process, attention purifies the heart and becomes prayer. The Greek fathers took advantage of the similarity between the words *prosoche* ("attention") and *proseuche* ("prayer") to demonstrate how closely the two realities are related to each other. "Attention that seeks prayer will find it, because prayer follows attention, and it is to the latter that we should apply ourselves" (Evagrius Ponticus); "Total attention is an aspect of continuous prayer" (Hesychius of Batos).

Closer to our time, Simone Weil, rephrasing Malebranche, has also spoken of attention in terms of prayer: "Attention, at its highest degree, is the same thing as prayer. It implies faith and love. Attention that is absolutely pure is prayer" (Weil 1962, 119). Such a condition of watchfulness and lucidity goes against all of the inclinations of the human mind that tend to debase it, such as laziness, drowsiness, negligence, superficiality, the scattering of one's thoughts, and *divertissement* ("distraction"). Because of the constant struggle it requires, attention is extremely difficult and costs us a great deal. Simone Weil continues, "There is something in our soul that shrinks from true attention much more violently than the body resists physical strain" (Weil 1966, 92). Through attention, our "I" is simplified and reduced to the essential: it "falls" and is drawn into the "object" of our desire. We realize, through our attention, that what makes us truly live is that upon which we focus our desire, longing, and love. Attention makes present the one who is longed for and desired. These words of St. Paul clarify what all of this means in Christian terms: "It is no longer I who live, but it is Christ who lives in me. And the life I now live in the flesh I live by faith in the Son of God, who loved me and gave himself for me" (Gal. 2:20).

14
LISTENING

ncapable of listening and speaking": this is humanity, according to a fragment of Heraclitus. Christians are fully aware that their ability to speak to their God, whom they cannot see, depends on listening to him. Faith comes from what is heard—*fides ex auditu* (Rom. 10:17), and prayer is first and foremost an act of listening: listening to God through the sacrament of his Word, Scripture, and listening to him in the world and in daily life, which becomes possible when prolonged contact with the gospel educates the believer's discernment. It is by listening that Christians learn to see. It should not surprise us, then, that Christianity is above all a discipline of listening, an *art of listening*. The New Testament asks us to pay attention to whom we listen to, how we listen, and what we listen to. This implies continuous discernment between words and the Word, the difficult task of recognizing God's word in human words and his will in historical events, and the attentiveness and availability of the entire human person.

We grow in the spiritual life to the extent that we descend into the depths of listening. Listening means not only confessing that another is present, but also making space in ourselves for this presence to the point that we become the dwelling place of the Other. The experience of the indwelling of the divine presence (the "visits of the Word" that St. Bernard acknowledged he had received several times following his biblical *lectio*) cannot be dissociated from our ability to "offer hospitality" to others by listening to them. This tells us that someone who listens, and who defines his or her identity on the basis of the paradigm of listening, is someone who loves—love also comes from what is heard, *amor ex auditu*. Our listening to God, with all of the dimensions this listening implies—silence, attention, interiorization, the spiritual effort of retaining what we have heard, the effort of decentering our attention from ourselves in order to recenter it on Another—leads us to welcome within ourselves a presence that is closer to us than our own "I"; or better, our listening leads to this presence's being revealed in us. We find ourselves reliving the experience of the patriarch Jacob, who exclaimed, "Surely, the Lord is in this place—and I did not know it!" (Gen. 28:16). The place where God is found is no other than the human being. In the Bible, God is not simply "the One who is"; he is also, and more significantly, "the One who speaks." By speaking, God seeks a relationship with each person and awakens our freedom, because if the Word is a gift, it can always be welcomed or refused. This is why reading is also an important spiritual discipline in Christian life: when we read, we meet the One who speaks through the biblical page. One of the terms used to designate the Bible in the Jewish tradition, *Miqra*, indicates a "call" to go out "from" and to travel "toward." From the perspective of faith, every act of reading the Bible is the beginning of an exodus in which we leave ourselves in order to meet Another—and this exodus takes place as we listen! Significantly, the biblical account of the exodus tells us that the great obstacle the people of Israel faced during their journey from

Egypt toward freedom was their own "hardness of heart": they were a "stiff-necked" people who persisted in listening not to God but to themselves. But it is also true that in the biblical experience of God and in the believer's own experience, there is the discovery that God is "the One who listens to prayer." Our own listening leads us to recognize God's listening as a dimension that precedes us and in which we are immersed. Paul says, "In him we live and move and have our being" (Acts 17:28). Listening is the contemplative, anti-idolatrous attitude par excellence. It is by listening that we seek to live consciously in the presence of God, the Other who is the origin of the irreducible mystery of all otherness. For Christians, listening is the source of life.

15

MEDITATION

I n early Christianity, the defining characteristic of Christian meditation was its application to and relationship with the Bible. This bond was broken, or at least weakened, during the centuries in which Scripture was exiled from the church, and during the *devotio moderna* period—and the Baroque era in particular—there was an efflorescence of *methods* of meditation. Increasingly schematic, complex, isolated, and considered authoritative points of reference in themselves, these methods were applied to subjects that became more and more detailed (saints' lives, theological doctrines, etc.), with the consequence that meditation became, in many instances, an artificial, complex act of rationalization, a purely intellectual and psychological exercise. These developments took place, significantly, during the historical period that witnessed the emergence of the "I" as a subject of reflection. In the Bible, the verb "to meditate" (*hagah* in Hebrew), which means "to murmur," "to whisper," or "to recite softly," is used with reference to the Torah, the written revelation of God's will. Biblical meditation is intended to lead those who practice it to understand God's will and to obey it by putting it into practice in their lives. The Latin verb *meditari* refers us to the idea of *exercise*, intended in the sense of repetition leading to the memorization and assimilation of a Word that we are asked not simply to understand, but to make incarnate in our lives. Meditation, then, is vital if our act of reading is to become an "incarnation" of the Word. Significantly, we find both in biblical terminology and in early Christian literature the idea of "eating" or "chewing" the Word, as a way of expressing the act of pondering the words of Scripture. As a result of linguistic convention, the Latin *exercere* is now used with reference to physical activity, while *meditari* is used with reference to spiritual activity, but meditation was understood in early Christianity as an activity that involved the entire personal self. "For the ancients, meditating meant reading a text and learning it by heart in the most profound sense of that act, with one's entire being: with the body because the mouth pronounces it, with the memory that grasps it, with the intelligence that understands its meaning, with the will that desires to put it into practice" (Leclerq 1965, 19–20).

This connection between meditation and the body, between prayerful reading and physical gestures, is clearly visible in Qur'anic and Talmudic schools, where the recitation of verses of Scripture is accompanied by rhythmic movements of the body and head. In Christian monasteries as well, there has always been an effort to unify reading and the body through the practice of *lectio divina*: the Word should imprint itself on the body! Hugh of St. Victor (twelfth century) distinguished *cogitatio*, conceptual analysis of the words one reads, from *meditatio*, which is identification and unification. Meditation thus begins with the act of reading, but evolves toward prayer and contemplation. We can understand why any discussion of Christian meditation leads us to the subject of *lectio divina*, the practice of reading-listening to Scripture in which our approach is not speculative but sapiential (wisdom-oriented) and respectful of the mystery the text contains. In *lectio divina* we first let the Word of God emerge from Scripture, and we then apply ourselves to the text and the text to ourselves in a dialogical process that becomes prayer and results in our living in conformity with the will of God expressed through the biblical page. The Christian tradition has described four steps in this process: *lectio, meditatio, oratio,* and *contemplatio.*

Meditation is the spiritual activity (generated by the Holy Spirit and involving the entire person, body and mind) that leads us from listening to the word to responding, in prayer and in our lives, to the God who makes his will known through the scriptural word. The centrality of the Bible in Christian meditation is not acciden-tal, but fully consistent with the nature of Christianity: God reveals himself by speaking, and his definitive revelation is the Word made flesh, Jesus Christ. For this reason, Christian meditation will always be a path of assimilation and interiorization of the Word of God. Scripture is a sacrament of this Word, but the Word also reaches us through our interactions with others and through the events of our lives, which we are also called to read, listen to, reflect on, and interpret. Through our meditation we give meaning to the events of our daily life, we discern the presence and Word of God in the world and in history, and we become capable of living in conformity with the Word. As we read the book of Scripture, we should also read the book of nature and the book of history. Christian meditation, then, does not consist in a technique, nor can it ever assign to the subject his or her own subjectivity as a goal. Rather, meditation always seeks to open us to alterity, love, and communion by guiding us toward the goal of having in ourselves the same attitude and will that were in Christ Jesus.

16

MEMORIA DEI

T wo biblical texts ask Christians to pray "always," "without ceasing." In the Gospel of Luke Jesus tells a parable about "the need to pray always and not to lose heart" (Lk. 18:1), and Paul commands, "Pray without ceasing" (1 Thess. 5:17). How is this possible? How can we reconcile this request with Paul's command to work (2 Thess. 3:12) and with his own example of working "night and day" (2 Thess. 3:8)? And how can one pray while sleeping?

These questions troubled early Christianity, monasticism in particular, and the attempts to respond were numerous. The Messalians, also known as the Euchites ("those who pray"), went to the extreme of refusing all work and claimed to devote themselves exclusively to prayer. Another attempt, equally extreme and equally futile, was that of the "acemetes" ("those who do not sleep"), who sought to dedicate themselves to prayer alone by reducing their sleep to an absolute minimum. Cenobitic monasteries, taking a different route, sought to multiply the number of liturgical "hours," and some monasteries created a form of continuous liturgical prayer, or *laus perennis*, by assigning rotations to different members of the community. Still other responses have focused on the inner life: repeating an invocation to God to the rhythm of one's breath and heartbeat, or even, as in the practice of so-called monological prayer, repeating tirelessly a single word, such as the name of Jesus.

The fruit of this focus of the believer's mind on the name of his or her Lord, this attention that empties the heart of all other thoughts so that the thought of God alone can dwell there, is the *mneme theou* or *memoria Dei*, the "remembrance of God." Described in particular in the spiritual teaching of Pseudo-Macarius, the "remembrance of God" is a profound spiritual act of unification of the heart in front of the interiorized presence of God. "Remembrance" is intended here in the sense of guarding in the heart—in other words, in the mind and the depths of the person—God's presence, and allowing one's exterior life to be unified and integrated with one's inner life in the light of this presence. This act of remembering becomes the light by which we live and reconsider the present, judging it in faith. *Memoria Dei* becomes the source of the discernment that produces spiritual wisdom and makes the believer capable of choosing each act and word in the light of the third person whom he or she makes reign in every relationship, God. The authoritative spiritual man or woman is brought into being by this life-giving *memoria*.

Memoria Dei is an act of remembrance that expresses love and desire for God, a profound attachment of the heart, and an awareness of his forgiveness. Pseudo-Macarius writes, "A Christian should always conserve the memory of God, because he or she should love God not only in church, but also while walking, speaking, and eating." This *memoria* becomes an *inner presence*, and this presence becomes prayer—life lived before God and in the awareness of his presence.

Through his or her *memoria* the believer is made the "dwelling of the Lord," as the apostle Paul affirms. It should be clear, then, that *memoria Dei* is not simply a psychological act; rather, it is the action of the Holy Spirit. The fourth Gospel, for which the Spirit has the function of "teaching and reminding" (John 14:26), tells us that the Spirit teaches us everything and reminds us of "all" that Jesus said and did. The Spirit appears here as a *memoria* of completeness, of a totality communicated not through the sum of Jesus's actions and words recorded in Scripture but through the presence of Jesus himself. It is a *memoria* of Jesus's words and silence, of the said and the unsaid, the fulfilled and the unfulfilled, the "already" and the "not yet," and therefore also of that which has not yet taken place. This remembrance, work of the Spirit, is also prophecy. It guides us toward that profound consonance with Christ, with what is at the source of his speaking and acting, that instills in us the ability to obey the gospel creatively, guided by the Spirit who makes Christ dwell in us. Concealed within *memoria Dei* is an attitude of gratitude and thanksgiving, faithfulness and commitment, self-surrender and hope. It is an act of remembrance that unifies the past, gives light and meaning to the present, and opens into expectation and hope for the future. We can understand why Gregory of Sinai (fourteenth century) claimed that the command "Remember the Lord your God at all times" is the most fundamental command of all: it is thanks to this commandment that all the other commandments can be fulfilled.

17
PRAYER, A JOURNEY

"There is no labor greater than prayer." How many young monks in the desert received this response from the elder or *abba* they had questioned. And the difficulty remains as time passes, though it assumes different nuances. Every generation, and each person in every generation, has the task of gathering together the legacy of prayer handed down to him or her and redefining it—and one can only redefine prayer if one prays! It is difficult today to understand the definition of prayer as an "elevation of the soul to God" that has traversed both the Christian East and West. After Auschwitz, many have asked whether it is still possible to pray at all. I think that the response to this question should not be limited to replacing the title given to God since the beginning, "Omnipotent," with the title "Impotent." (There are those who speak of the "all-weakness"—*omni-impotentia*—of God.) It seems to me that if we do this, we remain within the logic of theodicy. Instead, if we take seriously the fact that many at Auschwitz, as in so many other living hells, died praying, I think we can understand prayer as the believer's *journey toward his or her God*—or better, as his or her awareness of this journey. Christian prayer thus becomes the *space in which our images of God are purified*. It implies the difficult daily struggle of leaving behind our manufactured images of God in order to draw nearer to the God revealed in the crucified and risen Christ, the true image of God given to humanity.

If prayer is dialogue between God and a human being, a dialogue that implies the act of *listening* to the divine Word contained in Scripture and a human *response* (a response that also implies *responsibility*), we can also see it as a journey that awakens the person who prays to the dimension of communion, with God and with others. Prayer becomes our adaptation to the environment of the divine, life lived in the presence of God and with God, and a relationship with God. In prayer our heart—in other words, the center of who we are—is focused on the One who speaks to us and calls us, and we are decentered from ourselves and leave ourselves behind in the "ecstasy" (*ekstasis*) of meeting and knowing the Lord. This is how prayer happens: it is the believer's constant, unending journey toward his or her God, a God we never know completely when we begin, but with whom we have a relationship that *becomes* during the course of our life and our personal experience. This relationship never reaches a point of complete fulfillment, because prayer is a search for the face of God—the unceasing, insistent search of one who has been taken possession of by a Presence, even if the person who prays may never be able to find words to explain the ineffable experience that made him or her a believer.

Prayer, then, is an *awareness of Christian life as a journey toward God*: a God who is invisible and silent, but whose invisibility and silence are those of the Father. God is not absent; he is the Present One who conceals his presence in silence. He is the Father who, through his hiddenness and silence, makes his presence a call, a vocation. In this way prayer, a form of communication with One who remains silent and whom we do not see, releases our freedom and our human expression, allowing us to answer God's call and leading us toward knowledge of ourselves as we are led in our search for God. Our prayer to God is our answer to the prayer God addresses to us. We enter this dialogue with everything we are: as human beings we are longing, question, desire, relationship . . . and prayer expresses all of these dimensions, as thanksgiving, invocation, intercession, request. . . . The "guideline" for Christian prayer is the prayer of Jesus, the Son of God. In his own prayer Jesus experienced the nonfulfillment of the critical moment of Gethsemane, when he asked the Father to "let this hour" pass him by so that he might be spared the cup of bitterness, but he continued to abandon everything to the fulfillment of God's will, not his own. Prayer is not an exaltation of human desire, a request that God do our will, but rather the journey through which we come to recognize and accept God's will. Our knowledge of God continues to deepen, and our relationship with God changes as a consequence of what we know. Experience reveals that a person's experience of prayer changes over time. Only by changing can prayer continue to be a genuine relationship with God, a relationship that does not atrophy but remains living. The goal of this journey and this relationship is the conformity of our human life to the image of God, Jesus Christ.

18
LECTIO DIVINA

"The grace of God has appeared, saving all and training us . . . to live" (Titus 2:11–12). This New Testament passage speaks of Christ as grace personified, who teaches humanity to live. If the Spirit is the great instructor in Christian life, Scripture, a sacrament of the will and the Word of God, can be seen as the element that transmits the Spirit's teaching. Certainly, this refers to Scripture interpreted in the Holy Spirit, Scripture read in a spirit of prayer. *Lectio divina*, which finds its roots in the Jewish tradition of Bible reading and the patristic hermeneutic legacy, is the art of making the transition from a biblical text to our life. Because it helps us make this transition, *lectio divina* is a precious tool that can help us bridge the gulf we often observe in our churches between faith and life, spirituality and daily existence. It is an existential hermeneutic of Scripture that leads us, first, to turn our gaze toward Christ and search for him through the biblical page, and then to place our own existence in dialogue with the revealed presence of Christ and find our daily life illuminated, filled with new light. The four steps of *lectio divina*—*lectio, meditatio, oratio, contemplatio*—represent the progressive deepening of our understanding of the biblical text. Our act of reading becomes an encounter with the living Lord, dialogue with him, and the exposure of our life to the light of Christ, who gives order to our existence.

The process *lectio divina* sets in motion is a very human one: by listening we come to know, and by knowing we come to love. We begin by making the effort of "leaving ourselves" in order to bridge the chronological and cultural distance that separates us from the text: this allows us to accept the text in its otherness, as we would in any relationship with an other. During the next step, *meditatio*, we deepen our understanding of the text, search for its central message, and let the face of Christ emerge from the biblical page. In *oratio*, we apply the message that has come forth to our own life, considering our life in the light of the biblical message. *Oratio* is a response to the Word in the form of prayer, and it is also the moment in which we accept responsibility for the Word we have heard. Prayer and life take place on the same level; ethics and faith are not separate but intrinsically connected. In *lectio divina*, the Bible's dialogical intention meets the dialogical dimension of the person, which is a fundamental aspect of our human identity. The effectiveness of the Word of God contained in the Bible is revealed on the level of being, through who we are, much more and much sooner than it is revealed through our actions. This is the meaning of *contemplatio*, which refers not to mystical or ecstatic experiences but to a level of communication inexpressible in words: silence, tears, the presence of the lover to the beloved, discernment of the Lord's unutterable presence. *Contemplatio* also indicates the work accomplished in us by the Spirit who inhabits the Word: the Spirit creates in us patience, endurance, inner unification, discernment, a Eucharistic attitude, and compassion for all of creation—in a word, love that overflows.

This is essentially how *lectio divina* helps us make the transition between the Word and our life: it makes us people who know how to listen, and therefore people of faith.

In *lectio divina* our approach to the Bible is not intellectual but sapiential, and it obeys the principle of blessed Francis of Siena: "Anointing, not erudition; consciousness, not science; love, not the printed page." It is an approach to reading that requires *interiorization*, so that the Word can embed itself and take root in the human heart; *perseverance* in renewing day after day our willingness to listen and in standing firm in our faith, which embraces not just a certain phase of our life but our entire existence; and the *spiritual struggle* of clinging to the Word we have heard as we would to a precious possession, without exchanging it for those alluring but illusory goods that are actually idols.

In *lectio divina*, our reading of the Bible introduces us into the evangelically fruitful tension that accompanies conversion. *Lectio* leads the reader-listener to consider his or her own life in the light of God's will, revealed in Scripture, so that he or she can live according to the will of God. Our reading of the Bible is reflected in our life not primarily in the sense that our *lectio divina* leads us to choose certain actions over others, but because it illuminates and keeps burning in us the light that alone is capable of transforming all of our actions into testimony and evangelization: "Let your light shine before others, so that they may see your good works and give glory to your Father in heaven" (Matt. 5:16).

Scripture asks that we put into practice what we have read if we truly want to understand it, and it is in a community environment, together with others, that we are asked to do

this. "Many things in holy Scripture that I wasn't able to understand by myself, I understood by placing myself in front of my
brothers. . . . I realized that understanding had been granted
to me through them" (St. Gregory the Great). This is how the
transition from Scripture to life, from text to testimony, takes
place: Scripture, being inspired, also inspires and seeks to light
the fire of the Spirit in the believer's heart (see Lk. 24:32) so
that the Spirit can reveal his force in him or her. The reading
of Scripture gradually leads to our giving testimony (*martyria*)
to a Presence, and it finds its highest fulfillment in martyrdom,
the gift of one's life for love. Rabbi Akiva experienced his own
martyrdom as a fulfillment of the Shema: "You shall love the
Lord, your God, with all your life" (Deut. 6:5). As his torturers
were stripping his flesh from his body, Rabbi Akiva recited the
Shema, and when his disciples tried to interrupt him, he said,
"All my life I have thought about this verse: 'You shall love God
with all your life,' which means, you shall love him even if he
takes your life from you, and I said, 'When will I be able to do
that?' And now that I am able, should I not do it?" (*Babylonian
Talmud, Berakot* 61b).

The Word that has illuminated one's life transforms even death
into life. This awareness can help us answer an objection we often
encounter today in Christian environments, and that we can
express as follows: if the Word of God is effective, if Christians
are returning to the Word of God heard in Scripture, where can
we see this effectiveness? Where can we find signs of this power?
This objection reveals how difficult it is to take from Scripture,
and not from ourselves or the secular environment in which we

live, our criterion for judging effectiveness, which is the criterion of the cross. It is not by chance that Paul speaks of *ho logos ho tou staurou*, the "word of the cross" (1 Cor. 1:18), and yet this word, this effectiveness, is only perceptible and intelligible from within a perspective of faith. Only faith, moreover, can allow us to recognize the present ecclesial season of martyrdom as the fruit of the effectiveness of the Word, listened to and served to the point of giving one's life for love—love of God and others, love even for one's enemies and torturers.

19

CONTEMPLATION

ontemplation is a classic term in Christian vocabulary. It is also a word that has been abused—we often find it used to indicate a particularly elevated and "specialized" aspect of Christian experience, which is then contrasted with "active life" according to a schema that destroys the fundamental unity and simplicity of Christian experience. In the New Testament the word "contemplation," *theoria* in Greek, appears only once, in Lk. 23:48, with reference to Christ on the cross. "When all the people who had gathered for this spectacle [*theoria*, i.e., the Crucifixion] saw what had happened, they returned home, beating their breasts." The term designates here the *"concrete spectacle . . . of Jesus of Nazareth, the crucified 'King of the Jews'"* (Dossetti 1986, 223), and it is in relation to this permanent and irreducible focal center, Christ crucified, that the authenticity of Christian contemplation should be measured. We find a synonym for *theoria* in the New Testament, *gnosis*, "knowledge," or *epignosis* (literally, above-knowledge, i.e., spiritual knowledge): both of these terms appear more frequently than *theoria*. They also refer us to the centrality of the cross of Christ, true wellspring of Christian knowledge (see 1 Cor. 2:2), and therefore of Christian proclamation (1 Cor. 1:23) and praxis (Mk. 8:34). The cross, then, is at the heart of Christian contemplation. It inspires and regulates the content of faith ("not what I want, but what you want," Mk. 14:36) and the form faith should take in history ("not as I want, but as you want," Matt. 26:39).

Contemplation is by no means reserved for mystics or monastics—it is a reality to which all the baptized are called, because every baptized person has been immersed in life *in Christ* (Rom. 6:1–6) and clothed with Christ (Gal. 3:27), and Christian contemplation-knowledge has no other goal than that of making a Christian's personal and ecclesial life resemble the life of Christ. In contemplation, the crucified Christ makes his presence visible on the face of the one who prays and perceptible in the testimony of the individual and the entire ecclesial community. A contemplative is not someone who separates him- or herself from others or tries to escape society, but a person who tries to discern in history, in people, in events, and in his or her own person the presence of Christ. A contemplative's gaze searches deeply enough to recognize that the temple of God (the verb "to contemplate" refers us to *templum* and to the art of "looking at the contours of the temple"), the dwelling of the Holy Spirit, and the place where Christ lives is within the human being. The contemplative is an expert in the art of discerning God's presence, a presence not relegated to sacred places and not limited to the religious, but diffused everywhere.

Christian contemplation is an absorbing and outward-reaching activity that is capable of renewing our humanity and re-creating the human heart. "Show me your humanity, and I will show you your God," Theophilus of Antioch said. The perfect icon of God-humanity is the crucified Christ, who can be made known and visible to the world through the limitless compassion for those who suffer, the mercy, and the solidarity of Christians who know that they themselves are sinners. Contemplation of the crucified Christ immediately becomes vision of one's own sin and awareness that one truly is a sinner, and this leads to repentance and conversion: those who had contemplated Christ on the cross "returned home, beating their breasts" (Lk. 23:48). As Isaac the Syrian wrote, "One who sees his own sin is greater than one who sees angels." The goal of Christian contemplation is love, *makrothymia* ("patience, endurance"), compassion, and the opening outward of the heart. It is an event that does not "skip" the mediation of the church or the sacraments, and it is revealed when conversion becomes visible in a Christian's personal and community life.

We can go further. Christian contemplation sharpens our critical ability and makes us capable of evaluating history and the world in which we live. It is not by chance that John, who witnessed the crucifixion (see John 19:35–37), has become in Christian tradition the "visionary," the "theologian," and the "contemplative" par excellence. It is also significant that he has been credited with writing the book of Revelation, a text that is severe and penetrating in its criticism of the totalitarianism of the Roman Empire and that evaluates history through God's eyes, that is, with a spirit immersed in the gospel. Only profound familiarity with the gospel can produce a gaze capable of discerning human sin and God's presence in history. Christian contemplation springs from *listening to the Word*: it is rooted in the centrality of the Word of God in the believer's life, and in his or her faith that Scripture is a privileged form of mediation of this Word and of Christ's presence. It has been said that in Christian faith we "see through our ears"—in other words, *it is by listening that we arrive at contemplation.* This tells us that Christian contemplation takes place in the context of a relationship in which the initiative belongs to God, who "first loved us" (1 Jn. 4:19), who spoke to us first, and who has revealed in his Son the Word made flesh. This is the Word that is mediated through *Scripture* and passed from one generation to the next within the *Christian community*, where it is expressed as love. Radical acceptance of the Word leads to the *cross* (note again "the word of the cross" Paul speaks of in 1 Corinthians), and it is in the *company of others* that we give witness to the Word, proudly but with gentleness and respect. This is the Word from which Christian contemplation flows.

20

THE WORD OF THE CROSS

W hat has always been seen as the "scandal and foolishness" of Christianity is the event of the cross and, as a result, its metaphors and visual symbols. Christians face the temptation of "emptying the cross" of its meaning, as Paul points out in the First Letter to the Corinthians (1:17), and to those who are not Christian the cross and its logic appear inhuman or false as an attempt to respond to the problem of suffering. This has been true since the beginning of Christianity. But given the material well-being of those in the West today, the obsession with wealth and convenience, the search for pleasure without cost, and the conviction that everything that is technically possible and economically feasible is therefore legitimate and desirable, we have to admit that the removal of the cross is demonstrated daily in a thousand ways—some blatant, others extremely subtle—and that the foundation of Christianity seems to have faded into obscurity as a result. We might think of a number of examples to illustrate this: the attempt sometimes made today to present Christian life as if it were a constant celebration of the resurrection and nothing more, the amount of energy expended in an effort to present to young adults a gospel that is attractive because it has been liberated of every demand that involves discipline, self-denial, "renunciation" (an essential element of the baptismal liturgy, reduced today to an unpronounceable word), and the taking up of the cross, all expressions from the gospel considered "difficult" to speak about today. We might also think of the "Gnostic" speakers we encounter more and more often in ecclesial environments, who interpret Christian faith according to their own non-Christian criteria and present their listeners with a form of Christianity emptied of the "foolishness of the cross" and "enriched" with persuasive intellectual discourse.

Celsus is no longer the second-century philosopher who ridiculed Christians because of their Lord—a crucified criminal—and because of the church's extremely low sociological profile: the new Celsus proclaims Jesus a master of philanthropy and commends Christians who are visible and effective in the polis, but in doing so he relegates to obscurity the event that founded and that continues to inspire Christian life. At Celsus's side is the new emperor, who, like the one described by the great fourth-century church father Hilary of Poitiers, is underhanded in his flattery; instead of beating us on the back, he pats us on the stomach; instead of confiscating our wealth (and thus giving us life) he makes us wealthy, leading us toward death; he does not lead us toward freedom by putting us in prison, but toward slavery by inviting us into his palace and honoring us; instead of striking our body, he claims the heart; instead of beheading us with the sword, he kills our soul with money (*Liber contra Constantium* 5). This is how the cross, without being visibly or directly contested, is emptied of its meaning! Yet how insistently and forcefully John

Paul II asked Christians not to "empty the cross of Christ of its meaning"!

At least once a year, on Good Friday, the cross is placed in front of believers in all of its reality and truth: Jesus of Nazareth, a man, a rabbi, a prophet, is nailed completely nude to a block of wood. Crucified, he appears anathematized, excommunicated, not worthy of heaven or earth. He is abandoned by his disciples and dies scorned by those who witness his humiliating execution. This man is Jesus the *Just One*, who dies as he does because of the unjust world in which he lived; this man is a *faithful believer* in God, even if he dies the death of a sinner abandoned by God; he is the Son of God to whom the Father will respond with the Resurrection, making him pass from death to life.

And yet the event of the cross, which took place in Jerusalem on April 7 of the year 30 of our era, can also be emptied of its meaning through its metaphors and visual symbols, and as Christians we should be vigilant so that we do not end up like the "religious" people of every era who see the crucifixion as a scandal, or like the "wise" of this world who judge it foolishness. The cross is the "wisdom of God," and St. Paul, in coining the expression "the word of the cross" (1 Cor. 1:18), tells us that the event created by the cross is the gospel, the good news. Christians are not invited to respond to the cross with resignation, nor are they asked to think of suffering as having value in itself, or to make the cross their point of departure every time they think about the life of Jesus. They should realize, though, that Jesus's life and the form of his death, the crucifixion, were and are narrations of God: the living God who loves people even when they are evil, the God who forgives those who make themselves his enemies at the very moment when they reveal that they are enemies, the God who, in his desire that the sinner repent and live, allows himself to be rejected and killed. The cross, therefore, is also a denunciation of our sinfulness, our injustice, and our tendency to let ourselves be seduced by evil, since it is our evil that causes the Just One to suffer and be rejected, condemned and crucified. The cross has become the Christian emblem—at times exalted in a triumphalist way, other times reduced to a decorative ornament, a superstitious gesture, or a banal metaphor for simple daily adversity. Yet unless the cross remains a remembrance of the "instrument of our own execution," by which we put to death our "old self" (Rom. 6:6), it inevitably becomes a sign not inhabited by an event, and therefore a mystification. Martin Luther, meditating on the cross, echoed the church fathers when he wrote, "It is not enough to know God in his glory and majesty; it is necessary to know him in the humiliation and disgrace of the cross as well. . . . True theology and true knowledge of God are in Christ crucified."

21

PRAYER, A RELATIONSHIP

The prayer of every religious tradition, in its different forms and modes, is a direct reflection of the face of the God the believer of that tradition seeks to reach in prayer. And the God of biblical revelation is the living God we do not reach through our own reasoning, but who reveals, in the loving freedom of his actions, that he himself is in search of us. Far from being the fruit of a natural human sense of self-transcendence or the expression of an innate religious instinct, Christian prayer, which challenges every form of anthropocentric self-sufficiency, is our human response to God's free decision to enter into a relationship with us. It is God who, according to every page of the Bible, searches for, questions, and calls the human being, who is led from listening to faith and responds, in faith, by *giving thanks* (blessing, praise, etc.) and by expressing a request (invocation, supplication, intercession, etc.)—in other words, through prayer summarized in its two fundamental forms. Prayer is *oratio fidei* (Jas. 5:15), the eloquence of faith, an expression of personal attachment to the Lord.

Biblical revelation also attests that there is another dimension of prayer, the human search for God. Our search is the space we make available so that in it God can reveal himself to us, freely and according to his own initiative; it is our openness to meeting an other, essential if there is to be communion; it is our affirmation that God is indeed Other than us; and it is a sign of the fact that we cannot possess God, even when we know him. Searching is a fundamental aspect of the dialogue of love, the dialogical relationship that is central in prayer. If Christian prayer is a response to the God who has spoken to us first, it is also an invocation and search for the God who hides, who remains silent, who conceals his presence. The amorous dialogue in the Song of Songs, the game of concealment and disclosure, desire and pursuit between lover and beloved, can also be applied to prayer. We see this in the Psalms: "O God . . . I seek you . . . my soul thirsts for you . . . I think of you . . . in the watches of the night . . . My soul clings to you; your right hand upholds me" (Ps. 63). The dialogue of love in the Song of Songs is the fundamental reality toward which Scripture seeks to lead us in our relationship with God. This understanding of prayer as a relationship is perhaps what best expresses the proprium of Christian prayer, which introduces us into the covenant established by God with humanity and becomes a way of living within that covenant.

Having made these initial observations, we can say that just as life is adaptation to an environment, prayer, which is *spiritual life in action*, is our adaptation to our "ultimate" living environment, the reality of God in which everything and everyone is contained. Our essential point of departure in Christian prayer is the acceptance and confession of our weakness. We find such an attitude in the tax collector in the Lukan parable (18:9–14), who presents himself to God in prayer as he really is, without lies, masks, hypocrisy, or attempts at self-idealization, and who accepts what God thinks of him and how God sees him as the truth of who he is. Only those capable of a realistic attitude, an attitude of poverty and humility, can remain before God and allow themselves to be known as they really are. What is truly important, moreover, is the fact that we are known by God, because we know ourselves only in part (see 1 Cor. 13:12; Gal. 4:9). Our point of departure in prayer, then, is a confession of our inability to pray: "We do not know how to pray as we ought, but the Spirit himself intercedes with sighs too deep for words" (Rom. 8:26). This confession creates in us the openness that will allow us to welcome God's life within us. Prayer leads us to decenter ourselves from our own "I" so that our life can become more and more the life of Christ in us, and so that we can live as the Spirit guides us, as children of the Father. This decentering has nothing to do with the attempt to "make a void in oneself" that mimics spiritual practices belonging to other cultural and religious traditions. It is a decentering whose goal is agape, love. This goal of love, of leaving ourselves in order to meet the living person of Jesus Christ and come to love others "as he loved us," sets Christian prayer apart from forms of meditation and techniques of asceticism and concentration found in Asian religions. It is this understanding of prayer as a relationship, a relationship that reflects the life of the Trinity and that embraces both God and other people, that is the distinguishing feature of Christian prayer.

22

FIRST LISTEN

S peak, Lord, for your servant is listening" (1 Sam. 3:9): these words tell us that listening, according to Judeo-Christian revelation, is the fundamental attitude called for in prayer. They also contest a tendency we often have, despite our genuine desire to pray, to fill our prayer with such a flood of words that we effectively reduce God to silence. *Christian prayer is essentially an act of listening*: it is not the expression of a human desire for self-transcendence as much as the *welcoming of a presence* and a *relationship with an Other who precedes us and in whom we find our origin*. In the Bible God is not defined in abstract terms as "essence," but in terms of relationship and dialogue: he is first and foremost the One who speaks, and his initiative in speaking makes the believer *one who is called to listen*. The story of Moses's encounter with God at the burning bush (Exod. 3) is emblematic. Moses *draws near to look* at the remarkable sight of the bush that burns without being consumed, but God sees him *coming to look* and calls out to him from the bush, stopping him from drawing nearer. Vision is the domain of human initiative, in which we seek to reduce the distance between ourselves and God. It is the domain in which we make ourselves the protagonists and attempt to climb toward God. But the God who reveals himself introduces Moses into the domain of listening and maintains a distance between himself and Moses that cannot be crossed, because it is the distance that makes a relationship possible: "Come no closer!" (Exod. 3:5). What was a remarkable sight then becomes, for Moses, a familiar presence: "I am the God of your father" (Exod. 3:6). Unlike Prometheus, who climbs Mount Olympus to steal fire, Moses stops in front of the divine fire and listens to the Word. From that initial and initiating moment of listening onward, Moses's life and prayer become two inseparable aspects of his single responsibility to put into practice the word he has heard.

As we listen, God reveals to us that he is present even before we make our first effort to understand and perceive his presence. This tells us that *the one who truly prays is the one who listens*. "Listening is better than sacrifice" (1 Sam. 15:22)—better, in other words, than a relationship between God and a human being built on the fragile foundation of human initiative. If prayer is a dialogue that expresses our relationship with God, it is by listening that we are introduced into this relationship, this covenant, and this mutual belonging: "Listen to my voice, and I will be your God, and you shall be my people" (Jer. 7:23). We can see why the command to listen echoes throughout Scripture: it is by listening that we enter into the life of God, or better, that we allow God to enter our life. The great commandment *Shema' Israel* (Deut. 6:4–9), confirmed by Jesus as central in Scripture (Mk. 12:28–30), reveals that by *listening* ("Hear, O Israel"!) we come to *know* God ("The LORD is one"), and from knowing God comes *love* ("you shall love the LORD"). Listening, then, generates us as believers: it is the origin of prayer and of a life lived in relationship with the Lord. It is the dawning moment of faith (*fides ex auditu*: faith comes from what is heard, Rom. 10:17), and therefore of hope and love. Through listening we come into being. We become children of the Father, and it is not by chance that the New Testament points to Jesus, the Son, the Word made flesh, as the one who should be listened to: "Listen to him!" says the voice from the cloud on the Mountain of the Transfiguration, indicating Jesus (Mk. 9:7). Listening to the Son, we enter into a relationship with God, and in faith we can call him "Abba" (Rom. 8:15; Gal. 4:6) and "our Father" (Matt. 6:9)—listening generates us as children. As we listen, the efficacious Word and the re-creating Spirit of God penetrate us and become the principle of our transfiguration, our re-creation in the image of Christ. This is why we need "a listening heart" (1 Kgs. 3:9)—as we listen with our ears, it is our heart that listens! In the Bible the ear, which is not simply the organ of hearing but the seat of knowledge and the intellect, is directly related to the heart, the unifying center that embraces the emotional, rational, and volitional faculties of the person. As we listen, we acquire a heart that is "wise and understanding" (1 Kgs. 3:12), and we grow in discernment ("Let anyone who has an ear listen to what the Spirit is saying to the churches," Rev. 2:7). If listening is truly this central in the life of faith, it requires vigilance—in other words, watchfulness with regard to *what we listen to* (Mk. 4:24), *who we listen to* (Jer. 23:16; Matt. 24:4–6, 23; 2 Tim. 4:3–4), and *how we listen* (Lk. 8:18). In particular, we need to distinguish between words and the Word, give the Word precedence over the countless human words we hear, and listen with "an honest and good heart" (Lk. 8:15). What else does listening to the Word require? We find an answer in the explanation of the parable of the sower (Mk. 4:13–20; Lk. 8:11–15).

We need to know how to *interiorize* the Word, or it will remain ineffective and fail to produce the fruit of faith (Mk. 4:15; Lk. 8:12); we need to take time to listen and persevere in our listening, or the Word will not bear the fruit of stability, firmness, and depth of faith (Mk. 4:16–17; Lk. 8:13); we need to resist temptation by refusing the seduction of other worldly "messages" and "words," or the Word will be stifled, remain sterile, and fail to produce the fruit of maturity of faith (Mk. 4:18–19; Lk. 8:14). If we do not listen, we will find prayer impossible!

23

PRAYER AND THE
IMAGE OF GOD

n prayer we turn to the God we "have not seen" (see
1 Jn. 4:20)—and yet in prayer a certain image of God on the
part of the one who prays is necessarily involved. The risk of
falsehood and idolatry is evident: we run the risk of creating
for ourselves a God in our own image and likeness, and making
prayer an act of self-justification and self-reassurance in which
we remain closed within ourselves. The Lukan parable about the
prayer of the Pharisee and the tax collector at the temple (Lk. 18:9–
14) is significant. Their two different attitudes in prayer express
two different images of God related to the different images the two
men have of themselves. The Pharisee's prayer reveals the attitude
of someone who considers his conscience clear before God. His
God, in his eyes, cannot fail to praise his behavior, yet the last sentence of the narrative rejects his image of God—he does not return
home justified! While the tax collector exposes himself radically to
the alterity of God, and in so doing enters into a right relationship
with God, the Pharisee superimposes his "ego" on God's image: in
his prayer there is (con)fusion between his "I" and "God." For those
who are religious, this risk is a frequent one!

The centrality of listening in Christian prayer tells us that prayer
is the space in which the images of God we create are broken,

purified, and converted. In prayer two freedoms seek each other, human freedom and God's freedom. During this search, the gulf between the image of God created by the one who prays and God's revealed alterity becomes the distance between request and response, longing and fulfillment. This is why invocation is at the heart of Christian prayer: "Your will be done" (Matt. 6:10). Within the space that separates our will from the will of God, prayer acts as a site of conversion and acceptance of God's will. This is the distance, and the prayer, Jesus himself experienced at Gethsemane: "Abba, Father, for you all things are possible; remove this cup from me; yet not what I want but what you want" (Mk. 14:36). It is the distance, and the prayer, Paul experienced in a particularly dramatic way: "To keep me from being too elated by the exceptional character of the revelations, a thorn was given me in the flesh, a messenger of Satan, to torment me, to keep me from being too elated. Three times I appealed to the Lord about this, that it would leave me; but he said to me, 'My grace is sufficient for you, for power is made perfect in weakness'" (2 Cor. 12:7–9). Paul accepts the denial of his request, and his prayer leads him to reflect in his own existence the image of the God who does not give him what he asks but who remains beside him in his weakness. Paul has to accept the modification of his image of God, as correct and respectful as that image already was. In doing so, he allows his life to be conformed more and more fully to the revealed image of God, Christ crucified.

Christian prayer re-creates the one who prays in the image of the crucified Christ. And Christ, in his cry on the cross, accepted the total absence of images of God. The cry "My God, my God, why have you forsaken me?" (Mk. 15:34) proclaims the chasm between the familiar image of the face of God and the present reality. After Jesus's cry of abandonment, according to Mark, there is only another cry, this time inarticulate: "Jesus gave a loud cry and breathed his last" (Mk. 15:37). There is no longer any word or image; there is no longer any theology; there is no longer any word about God; there is no longer any representation of God. As a result, there is no longer any reduction of God to an idol! The three hours of *silence* and darkness from the sixth to the ninth hour are the seal of this wordlessness and invisibility of God who safeguards his mystery and his alterity.

But it is precisely this radical annihilation of images of God (who has ever thought to depict God in a condemned criminal?) and words about God (what logos is not broken in two by God crucified?) that is also a radical abolition of idolatry, of our reduction of God to our image. It is in Christ on the cross that we now find the presence and image of God: "He is the image of the invisible God" (Col. 1:15). *The crucified Christ annihilates God as man's image and gives us a man who is the image* (eikon) *of God*. Christ on the cross is the image of God that destroys our images of God. The crucified Christ is also the image before which we pray, but who must destroy the images we project, intentionally or despite our best intentions, onto God. The image of God revealed by Christ on the cross contradicts the image of God "professed" by the Pharisee at the temple—an image connected to a certain consideration of himself supported by a derogatory image of others. In prayer, then, we "compose" our images of ourselves, of others, and of God around the crucified Christ. The image of God that is Christ on the cross preserves Paul from the temptation of pride and from his own "superego":

his "being too elated" (*hyperairomai*, 2 Cor. 12:7) is converted into boasting of the sufferings he has endured for the sake of Christ (*hyper Christou*, 2 Cor. 12:10). Through prayer, Paul participates in the suffering of Christ: "I carry the marks of Jesus branded on my body" (Gal. 6:17; cf. Col. 1:24). As prayer transforms those who pray into the image of Christ crucified, it also becomes a promise of resurrection and the space in which we are transfigured in the image of the Lord in glory (see 2 Cor. 3:18).

24

PRAYER OF INTERCESSION

n prayer we carry our entire life with us. We are beings-in-relationship with others: other people are part of us, and our relationships play a central role in determining who we are and who we will become. As we address God the Father in prayer as his sons and daughters, we are also confirmed in our fellowship with others. Intercession is the form of prayer that most clearly reveals the fullness of our existence in relationship to God and other people. It also reveals the profound unity between responsibility, social involvement, love, justice, and solidarity on the one hand, and prayer on the other hand. What does the word *intercede* actually mean? *Intercedere* means "to step between" or "mediate" between two parties. It therefore indicates an active commitment on our part in which we take our relationships with others as seriously as we take our relationship with God. In particular, it means taking a step toward someone in favor of someone else. Paraphrasing Psalm 85:10, we might say that in intercession "faith and love meet," "faith in God and love for humanity embrace each other." Intercession does not lead us to remind God of others' needs, since he knows what we need (see Matt. 6:32). Rather, it leads us to open ourselves to another person's needs by remembering that person in the presence of God and receiving him or her again from God, illuminated in the light of the divine will.

This double movement, this stepping from humanity to God and from God to humanity, bound both by obedience to God's will for ourselves, others, and the world and by compassion for others in their situations of sin, need, and poverty, explains why intercession in the Bible is the special responsibility of the pastor or leader of the people, the king, the priest, and the prophet. Intercession finds its full realization in Christ, the "one mediator between God and humankind" (1 Tim. 2:5). It is with Christ, and him crucified, that Job's longing is fulfilled: "If only there were someone between us, Lord, who might lay his hand on us both, on my shoulder and on your shoulder" (Job 9:33). Here Job is asking for an intercessor! If the icon of the intercessor in the Old Testament is Moses who, standing on the hill between Aaron and Hur, who support his hands, keeps his arms raised toward heaven to ensure the victory of the people of Israel fighting on the plain (Exod. 17:8–16), in the New Testament the icon of the intercessor is the crucified Christ, whose arms outstretched on the cross lift all of humanity up to God. Christ on the cross lays one hand on God's shoulder and the other hand on each human shoulder. The most complete act of intercession is thus the gift of one's life, the taking of another person's place, the cross! Moses expresses this well in his intercession for the children of Israel: "Lord, if you will only forgive their sin—but if not, blot me out of the book that you have written" (Exod. 32:32). In our intercession we learn to offer ourselves to God for the sake of others, and to express this act of offering in a concrete way in our daily lives.

Intercession leads us to the heart of what it means to live a responsible Christian life. In total solidarity with others in their sin and need, knowing that we ourselves are in the same condition of sin and need, we step into a human situation in communion with God, who in Christ has taken the decisive step for the salvation of all people. The Servant of the Lord intercedes for sinners by taking upon himself their sin and the punishment intended for them, and bearing their infirmity and weakness (Isa. 53:12). Through his Incarnation and death on the cross, Christ accomplished the most radical act of intercession possible, the decisive step between God and humanity. Now, living for ever with God, he continues to intercede for us as a great and merciful high priest (Heb. 7:25). His hand on our shoulder inspires our trust, boldness, and *parrhesia*: "Who is to condemn? Is it Christ Jesus, who died, yes, who was raised, who is at the right hand of God, who indeed intercedes for us?" (Rom. 8:34). The gift of the Spirit makes us participants in the intercession of Christ: the Spirit teaches us to pray "according to the will of God" (Rom. 8:26–27), conforming our prayer and our life to the prayer and life of Christ. It is only in the Spirit, who tears us away from our closed individuality, that we are able to pray for others, allow them to dwell within us, and lift them up into the presence of God. In the Spirit we even find it possible to pray for our enemies, which is an essential step to take if we want to learn to love our enemies (Matt. 5:44).

There is direct reciprocity between prayer for others and love for others. We might say, in fact, that the fullest expression of our intercession consists less in words spoken before God than in living in the presence of God in the position of the crucified Christ, with outstretched arms, in faithfulness to God and in solidarity with humanity. And at times there is absolutely nothing else we can do, when we want to preserve a relationship with another person, except preserve the relationship in our prayer and intercession. At this point it should be clear that intercession is not a task, a duty, or "something we should do," but the essence of a life consumed by love for God and others. The church should remember this: what is the church if it is not intercession with God for all people? This is the truly powerful service the church is called to carry out in the world. It is a service that situates the church in the world not as the leader of crusades, but as a body that bears the marks of the cross!

25

PRAYING WITHIN HISTORY

t may puzzle or irritate some, but every time a war breaks out the successor of Peter, the pope, asks Christians to pray insistently so that pathways of peace, dialogue, and then reconciliation might be opened; bishops and pastors of other Christian denominations also call for prayer; Christians of all ages, men and women from every corner of the globe, turn to their God, Father of all, in a heartfelt prayer of intercession. Is this a useless rite? A pacifying refuge for the conscience? No, prayer itself is the eloquence of their faith: if there were no prayer—no addressing God as "you"—there would be no faith, no trust placed in God, no adherence to the living Lord. For Christians, prayer is action par excellence, "work that needs to be done," praxis, activity that is effective within history.

In times of war, we quickly discover the extent of our own powerlessness and our inability to arrive at a clear understanding of the reasons behind a conflict. Almost daily we hear a denunciation of the twentieth century as a century steeped in blood, but even today we find ourselves facing situations that evoke the beginning of the last century. But it is precisely when Christians discover the extent of their own powerlessness that they turn to the Lord: not to invoke magic solutions, evade involvement and responsibility, or refuse to take part in history, but because their faith in the Lord of history moves them to intercede. "To intercede" means "to step between" one reality and another, to introduce into a negative situation elements capable of bringing about a change in the situation. It means expressing solidarity with those in need, helping them to the extent that our ability and our understanding of the situation permit, and above all fulfilling the will of the Lord, which is always forgiveness, peace, and fullness of life. Jesus said, "If you, who are evil, know how to give good gifts to your children, how much more will the heavenly Father give the Holy Spirit to those who ask him!" (Lk. 11:13). This is the "good gift" Christians ask for in prayer: the Holy Spirit who acts in the hearts and minds of all people, inspiring thoughts and plans of peace. This is what Christians can be sure they will obtain, because it was Jesus's promise.

Guided by the Spirit, our prayer truly does become effective in history: in it we gather together the voices of all of the world's victims and their cries for justice. Our prayer becomes the voice of all of the innocent blood poured out during the course of history, from that of the righteous Abel to the blood of the world's poor, of those unarmed Kosovars, Albanians, or Serbs who have been victims of violence and of a war planned by others—a war from which no victor can emerge, but only men and women who have been defeated, disfigured for generations by the brutality of one human being's violence against another. Prayer is an essential component of history because the cry of the poor and the world's victims, which ascends to God as a plea for justice and peace, is never lost. As Jesus said, "Will not God grant justice to his chosen ones, who cry to him day and night?" (Lk. 18:7). Those who consider prayer an evasion of history or an easy answer show that they do not know the meaning of hope and expectation, and that they experience the succession of historical events as an eternal continuum governed by fatalism and cynicism. When the successor of Peter asks the church to pray, what he asks is that the church act in a way that is as consistent as possible with its faith, and that it be present in the world with the only arms it possesses, the arms of intercession that have the power to save. He asks the church to be present in the world without being worldly, and to let its actions be inspired by listening to the Word of God. As the psalmist says: "Let me hear what God the Lord will speak, for he will speak peace to his people, to his faithful, so that they do not return to their madness!" (Ps. 85:9).

Without prayer one may have a vague sense of belonging to Christianity, but instead of authentic faith, there is only ideology; instead of hope, there is self-sufficiency; instead of Christian love, there is only frenzied philanthropic activity driven by a desire for visibility. Even when appearances seem to demonstrate the contrary, prayer—dialogue with the God who saves—will save the world.

26
PRAYER OF REQUEST

form of prayer most frequently attested in Scripture, and taught by Jesus himself (see Matt. 7:7–11; 21:22), is the prayer of request. This is also the form of prayer that has caused more problems in the Christian tradition than any other. Christian writers have often spoken of the greater purity and perfection, and the overall superiority, of the prayer of praise and thanksgiving: "The principal form of prayer is thanksgiving," wrote Clement of Alexandria in the third century (*Stromata* 7.79.2). Much closer to our era, and in the 1960s and 1970s in particular, the prayer of request underwent a serious crisis. The process of secularization then underway, as well as the growing mastery, through science and technology, of areas that had long evaded human comprehension and had been delegated to the intervention of God, caused the prayer of request to be set aside as superfluous. Today we are observing its reemergence, often in forms that are not faithful to the gospel and that reduce this prayer to a request for a "magical" intervention, or, at times, to a demand addressed to a God who is seen as immediately "available," a God whose duty it is to satisfy every need. To begin, it should be said that from an anthropological point of view human beings do not simply make requests: the human being *is* a request, an appeal. This dimension of who we are always reveals itself in prayer, because in prayer, "whatever the specific circumstance happens to be, one's entire being is placed before God" (Ott 1991, 52). As we turn to God with our requests in the different situations of our life, we express our desire—without setting aside in the least our own responsibilities and commitments—to receive again and again our identity and the meaning of our life from God, in the context of our relationship with him. We confess that our life does not "belong" to us and is not simply our own. In this sense the prayer of request is unquestionably scandalous—it is an affront to our pretenses of self-sufficiency. Further, behind every authentically Christian prayer of request there is a radical request for meaning. This is a search that technological progress will never be able to make outdated, and it directly concerns not only the believer ("Who am I?") but also the God in whom "we live and move and have our being" (Acts 17:28). In our prayer of request we rise above our need and transfigure it in desire. We place a certain distance between ourselves and our situation, establish a period of waiting between our need and its satisfaction, and try to make space for an Other within the enigmatic situation in which we are living.

This makes the prayer of request eminently contemplative: it is the believer's way of affirming that God is truly Lord of the world and of all creation. A believer who asks something of God is more interested in God's presence than in obtaining a particular benefit. The prayer of request is comprehensible and possible only in the context of a relationship in which we address God as his sons and daughters (Matt. 7:7–11), and such a relationship is only possible in faith (Rom. 8:14–17). It is within this relationship and this faith, and within the limits of both, that the Christian prayer of request finds its meaning. It should by no means be confused with forms of the prayer of request found in other religions, but finds its *norma normans* in the order of the requests made in the Our Father, where everything is centered on the request "Your kingdom come." Our criterion for measuring the authenticity of our prayer is the prayer of request the Son Jesus Christ addresses to his Father. Jesus's faith and his filial relationship with God, his way of addressing his Father, are offered as a model for the believer's prayer of request. The experience at Gethsemane is significant: Jesus confesses God as "Abba, Father" (Mk. 14:36) and in the intimacy of his relationship with God asks that "the hour" (Mk. 14:35) and "this cup" (Matt. 26:39) pass by him, but he subordinates his request to "not *what* I want but what you want" (Mk. 14:36); "not as I want, but *as* you want" (Matt. 26:39). There is therefore a content (*what*) and a form (*as*) that are summarized in the *cross* and represent the limit we encounter in the Christian prayer of request. This is a prayer that can take the form of a struggle between the believer and his or her God, a confrontation and interaction between two freedoms. It is important to safeguard the freedom of the one who prays, and thus his or her freedom in asking; God's freedom, and thus his freedom in answering; the autonomy of natural laws and the other realities of the physical world; and the reality of God's spiritual presence in the world. From a Christian perspective, the prayer of request is not a magical means of resolving the enigmas of human existence or avoiding what is negative in life. In our relationship with God there is a dimension of enigma that cannot be removed ("My God, my God, why have you forsaken me?," Mk. 15:34), but that can transform itself into mystery during prayer. The Bible suggests an approach to the prayer of request in which we begin by recognizing that "we do not know how to pray" (Rom. 8:26). In each person's experience of prayer there is an apprenticeship: as the years pass we learn how to ask, we grow in our relationship with the Lord, and we learn to make our requests "in the name of the Lord" (John 14:13–14) and not in our own name. In other words, we learn to exercise discernment with regard to our needs, to know the Lord, and to remember the need for constant conversion to the will of God expressed in his Word. We do not reach our aim in the prayer of request when God does our will, but when we do his will (Matt. 6:10)! Our prayer requires faith: "Whatever you ask for in prayer, believe that you have received it, and it will be yours" (Mk. 11:24). The gift is given before we ask for it; God's response comes before our request! What God has already given us is the gift of his Son Jesus Christ! Dietrich Bonhoeffer writes: "Everything we should ask of God and hope to receive from him is in Jesus Christ. We should try to enter into Jesus' life, words, actions, suffering, and death, so that we can recognize what God has promised and what he always does for us. God does not give us everything we desire, but he keeps his promises. He is still the Lord of the earth who protects his church, continues to renew our strength, and does not impose burdens on us beyond what we can bear, but fills us with his presence and strength" (Bonhoeffer 1973, 396, 401). Here we see clearly the importance of the prayer of request, and at the same time, the need for it to be constantly purified and made more faithful to the gospel.

27

PRAYER OF PRAISE

hristian prayer takes place between the two poles of lament and praise. It is particularly difficult, I find, to speak about the prayer of praise. It reaches us burdened with a judgment of excellence compared to other forms of prayer, a judgment formulated repeatedly by the Christian tradition on the basis of its supposed purity, and its disinterested and gratuitous nature. I find the logic that generates comparisons and judgments of superiority and inferiority inappropriate here, precisely because praise, being gratuitous, can be better understood if we remember that prayer is essentially relationship and dialogue. Praise and request complement each other in prayer, and it is their polarity and complementarity that make the relationship that is prayer balanced and authentic. Prayer is not simply a series of demands (which it would be if it were exclusively request), nor is it flattery (which it would be if it were exclusively praise). It is a real (and not ideal) encounter that takes place between a human being and God, within history and in the concreteness of daily life. In prayer, God makes himself present in a human life by revealing the wonders of his love and inspiring the response of praise; at other times, he conceals himself behind the enigmas of suffering, death, and distress, provoking a request, lament, or supplication.

In human interpersonal relationships praise is the language that expresses acceptance and a positive view of another person— usually it is the language of lovers. In prayer, we might call praise love answering love. We respond to the love of God that we have recognized in the events of our life with praise, acknowledging the Other in the greatness of his works and gifts. Praise is always a response to the person of God, and not to his gifts: the prayer of praise is theocentric. It is our "amen," our "yes" to God and his actions, and it is a "yes" that is total and unconditional. This is the praise Jesus himself offered: "I thank you, Father, Lord of heaven and earth, because you have hidden these things from the wise and the intelligent and have revealed them to infants; yes, Father, for such was your gracious will" (Matt. 11:25–26). The Christian's praise repeats this movement, finding its catalyst in Christ: "For in him every one of God's promises is a 'Yes.' For this reason it is through him that we say the 'Amen,' to the glory of God" (2 Cor. 1:20). In the liturgy, the authoritative source of Christian prayer, the Easter season is marked by the constant repetition of the exclamation "Alleluia" ("praise the Lord"). In this way the liturgy shows us that God's great gift is the Son himself, who died and rose again for the salvation of humanity. It is the saving action of the triune God, fully revealed through the paschal event, that inspires the doxology, the praise of the church.

This aspect of praise as an "Amen" addressed to God, a confession of his alterity and presence, shows us how closely praise is related to belief: praise expresses the celebratory aspect of faith. It is significant that in the Bible, praise often springs from discernment, in faith, of an intervention of God in history. An example of this is the canticle of Moses, which follows his confession of God's intervention in leading the people of Israel out of Egypt (see Exod. 15). Rather than calling praise superior to supplication, we should place supplication under the overarching horizon of praise. *Supplication implies praise and evolves in the direction of praise.* Its foundation is praise, since in supplication the believer confesses and invokes the Name of God, and recognizes that he or she cannot turn to anyone else except to the God who has abandoned him or her ("My God, my God, why have you forsaken me?," Ps. 22:1). It evolves toward praise because the one who prays hopes to see again the face of the Lord he or she knows and loves. This explains why the psalms of lament often end with an expression of praise (e.g., Pss. 22, 31, 69), and why the psalmist, as he laments his exile or his distance from God, can still exclaim, "I shall again praise him" (Pss. 42:6, 12; 43:5). This aspect of hope, of future praise, is particularly evident in the doxologies we find in the book of Revelation, which describe eternal life as filled with the praise of believers. What is affirmed here is a future *relationship of presence* in which there will no longer be any shadow to separate the believer from his or her God. If praise brings together in prayer the dimensions of faith, hope, and love, it is clear that it is the substance of our life, the way we are called to live. We are destined to be "praise of God's glory" (Eph. 1:14), and our life itself should become praise. Those who love God with all their heart, and their neighbor as themselves, want to give praise with all their heart by living and dying in God's presence.

Significantly, the Christian tradition presents the martyr as an example of praise expressed in an entire life up until the very end, almost an "amen" personified. The fundamental importance of praise in prayer explains why praise finds so many different linguistic forms of expression in our personal and community life. From song to whispered or murmured words, from joyful celebration to inner exultation, from words to silence: "Even silence praises you, O God" (Ps. 65:2). In silence, praise becomes the *cor ad cor* presence of beloved to Lover.

28

PRAYER OF THANKSGIVING

n the Gospel episode of the ten men with leprosy healed by Jesus (Lk. 17:11–19), we are told that to only one of them the Lord says, "Your faith has made you well" (Lk. 17:19): it is the one who realizes that he has been healed and returns to thank Jesus. Christian faith is Eucharistic, and only those who give thanks experience the reality of salvation—in other words, the reality of God's actions in their lives. Since faith is a personal relationship with God that embraces one's entire life, giving thanks is not just a question of saying certain prayers. Our entire existence should become thanksgiving. This is what Paul says: "Be Eucharistic!" (Col. 3:15).

As fundamental as it is, giving thanks is by no means easy! From an anthropological point of view, it is a language that is not spontaneous in young children. Giving thanks implies a sense of alterity, the crisis of our narcissism, and the ability to enter into a relationship with another, a "you": it is only to another person that we say "thank you"! Those who are grateful are those who have put to death their image of themselves as someone who "owes nothing to anyone," and who have realized that they cannot manipulate reality and other people as they please. In our relationship with God, our "Eucharistic" ability is a sign of the maturity of our faith. We give thanks when we acknowledge that "everything is grace," and that God's love goes before us, accompanies us, and follows us in our lives. Thanksgiving flows naturally from the central event in Christian faith: the gift of the Son Jesus Christ that God the Father, in his immense love, has made to humanity (see John 3:16). This is the saving gift that inspires our thanksgiving and makes the Eucharist the church's action par excellence. "It is right to give you thanks and praise always and everywhere, all-powerful and eternal God, through Jesus Christ our Lord." These words from the Eucharistic prayer in the Roman Missal describe Christian thanksgiving as unceasing. Since the Eucharist (and in particular the Eucharistic prayer) is the model for Christian prayer, Christians are called to make their entire life an occasion for giving thanks. As Paul says, "What do you have that you did not receive?" (1 Cor. 4:7). The human response to God's freely given gift is *acknowledgment* of the gift and gratitude. We might call even human thanksgiving a gift of God: "We owe gratitude to God for the gift of gratitude," goes a prayer in the Jewish liturgy.

Giving thanks is therefore the Christian's own spiritual mode, his or her way of interacting with the world, with objects, and with others. This explains why a gesture as basic and vital as the sharing of a daily meal is always accompanied by a prayer of thanksgiving. Giving thanks to God at the beginning of a meal ("saying grace" or "saying the blessing") is a confession of faith in which we acknowledge that both life and its meaning are a gift of God. We are granted life through the food we eat, and the meaning of life is represented by the relationships and the conviviality that unite those who have come together around the table. In the Eucharist, life and the meaning of life are present in the person of the living Christ, who gives himself as food of eternal life and renews the relationships of communion that join the members of the assembly. When a Christian receives the gift of fullness of life in the Son, he or she responds by giving thanks for having been created and for having received the gift of faith. A traditional morning prayer says, "I adore you, my God, and I love you with all my heart. I thank you for creating me, making me a Christian, and watching over me during this night."

We respond to the gift of God above all by making our own life a gift, an act of thanksgiving, a living Eucharist. The prayer of thanksgiving truly is much more than our timely response to events in which we discern God's presence and action in our lives. It is an inner orientation of our existence, the exposure of our daily life to the transfiguration of the coming kingdom of God. It results in even death being transfigured and becoming an event of birth to new life. At the moment of his martyrdom, Cyprian of Carthage's last words were *Deo gratias;* John Chrysostom ended his difficult existence with the same words of thanksgiving to God; Clare of Assisi, as she took her last breath, prayed, "Thank you, Lord, for creating me." These Christians made the conclusion of their lives a Eucharist. It is true that the prayer of thanksgiving considers the past and what God has done for us; it is "retrospective" and flows from what we remember. But this prayer is also one that opens into hope for the future, and it is a specifically Christian way of living in the present, which is itself the space in which we live.

29

SILENCE

The spiritual and ascetic tradition has always seen silence as essential to an authentic spiritual and prayer life. "The father of prayer is silence, the mother of prayer is solitude," Girolamo Savonarola said. Silence alone makes listening possible—in other words, it alone allows us to welcome within us not only the Word but also the presence of the One who speaks. Through silence we awaken to the experience of the indwelling of God, because the God we seek by following the risen Christ in faith is a God who is not outside of us, but who dwells within us. In the fourth Gospel Jesus says, "Those who love me will keep my word, and my Father will love them, and we will come to them and make our home with them" (John 14:23). Silence is a language of love, of depth, of being present to another. In the experience of love, it is a language that is often much more eloquent, intense, and communicative than a word.

Today, unfortunately, silence is rare. It is what most is missing in a world in which we are deafened by noise, bombarded by visual and auditory messages, and bereft of—at times almost exiled from—our interiority. It is not surprising, then, that "when the prestige of language diminishes, that of silence increases" (Sontag 1975, 20). Spiritual life as well shows signs of a lack of silence: today's liturgies are often heavily verbal, weighed down by texts that, by seeking to explain all and say all, forget that in God there is a dimension of wordlessness, silence, and mystery that the liturgy should reflect. The growing demand for authentic spiritual life is too often neglected by local churches that are involved instead in countless social, charitable, recreational, and catechetical activities. Given this situation, the widespread interest today in forms of spirituality that are not Christian should not surprise us.

We need to recognize our need for silence! We need silence from a purely anthropological point of view, because we are social beings, and only a harmonious relationship between words and silence makes our communication well-balanced and significant. From a spiritual point of view as well, though, we need silence. In Christianity, silence is a dimension of our humanity, but also a theological dimension. Alone on Mount Horeb, the prophet Elijah hears first a strong wind, followed by an earthquake and then a fire, and finally "a sound of sheer silence" (1 Kgs. 19:12). When he hears this, Elijah hides his face in his cloak and steps into the presence of God. God reveals his presence to Elijah in a silence that is eloquent, and elsewhere in the Bible the revelation of God is communicated not only with words but also in silence. For Ignatius of Antioch, Christ is "the Word that proceeds from silence." The God who reveals himself in silence and through the Word asks human beings to listen, and in order to listen we need silence. Of course, refraining from speaking is not enough— we also need interior silence, that dimension that restores us to ourselves and places us on the level of being, face-to-face with what is essential. "Inherent in silence is a marvelous power of observation, clarification, and concentration on the things that are essential" (Bonhoeffer 1969, 104). It is from silence that an acute, penetrating, judicious, and luminous word can arise, a word that we might also call therapeutic, capable of offering consolation. Silence is the guardian of interiority. Yes, we are speaking about a silence that can be defined in negative terms as moderation and restraint in speaking, or even as abstention from speaking, but from here we move toward an interior dimension in which we also silence the thoughts, images, protests, judgments, and complaints that arise in the heart: "It is from within, from the human heart, that evil intentions come" (Mk. 7:21). This is the difficult interior silence that must be sought and pursued within the heart, the site of the spiritual struggle. Yet it is this profound silence that generates love, empathy, attentiveness toward others, and the ability to welcome them. Silence creates a space deep within us so that in it the Other can dwell and his Word remain. In this space, love for the Lord is rooted deeply in us. At the same time, interior silence makes us capable of listening intelligently, speaking with discretion, and discerning what burns in the heart of another, concealed in the silence from which his or her words arise. Silence, this silence, becomes the source of our love for others. This is why the double commandment of love for God and for our neighbor can be fulfilled by those who know how to be silent. Basil says, "A silent person becomes a source of grace for those who listen." At this point we can recall, without the risk of cliché, the words of E. Rostand: "Silence is the most perfect song, the highest prayer." If our silence leads us to listen to God and love others with genuine love—if, in other words, it leads us to life in Christ, and not to a generic and sterile inner void—then it is an authentically Christian form of prayer and pleases God.

This interior silence has a long spiritual history. It is the silence practiced by hesychasts in their search for unification of the heart; it is the silence of the monastic tradition, a silence that allows those who practice it to welcome within themselves the Word of God; it is the silence of the prayer of adoration of God's presence; it is the silence treasured by mystics of every religious tradition. Even more fundamentally, it is the silence that saturates poetic language, the silence that is the substance of music, the silence that is essential to every act of communication. Silence, an event of depth and unification, makes the body eloquent by guiding us to the *habitare secum* so highly valued by the monastic tradition, in which we learn to inhabit our body and our inner life. Inhabited by silence, the body becomes a revelation of the person.

In Christianity we contemplate Jesus Christ as the Word made flesh, but also as the Silence of God. The Gospels show us a Jesus who, as he goes toward the passion, increasingly refrains from speaking and enters into silence, like a mute lamb. One who knows the truth and the inexpressible ground of reality neither wants nor is able to betray the ineffable in speech, but protects it with his silence. Jesus, who "does not open his mouth" (Isa. 53:7), reveals that silence is what is truly strong. He makes his silence an action, and by doing so he is also able to make his death an act, the gesture of a living person. In this context it should be clear that behind both words and silence, what truly saves is the love that gives life to both. Who is the crucified Christ if not the icon of silence, the silence of God himself? The Gospels tell us that from noon until three o'clock in the afternoon, the hour of Christ's death on the cross, darkness and silence reign. All words about God, images, conceptualizations, and ideas about God are silent. It is against this silence that we should measure theology, every discussion about God, and every representation of God, because we always face the temptation to reduce God to an idol, a manufactured object that can be manipulated. The silence of the moment of the cross is able to express the inexpressible: the image of the invisible God is found in a man nailed to a cross. The silence of the cross is the authoritative source from which every theological word should be drawn.

30

CHASTITY

Speaking about chastity is not easy. It is a word, and a reality, often understood in a reductive way or even misunderstood and ridiculed; at times, it is confused with virginity or identified with sexual abstinence. Rediscovering the anthropological value of chastity can help us rediscover its spiritual value in Christian life. The word's background suggests that a chaste person (*castus*) is one who refuses incest (*incastus*)—a person who is not chaste, etymologically, is incestuous. A chaste person accepts distance and respects alterity (which cannot be reduced to difference) in his or her relationships; a person who is not chaste seeks not a relationship but the fusion and confusion that normally define incest. This basic definition makes chastity part of the art of learning to love and express one's sexuality in a mature and adult way. This does not make it a negative virtue, marked by prohibitions, but one that is eminently positive and that "gives human relationships their sincerity and warmth, and allows people to recognize one another in the respect of their inmost self " (Flipo 1992, 168). J. Gründel writes, "Chastity is the inner availability that allows a person to affirm fully his or her own sexuality, recognize the personal and social nature of sexual impulses, and give them a meaningful place within human life as a whole." Chastity is "well-ordered love [*amor ordinatus*] that does not subordinate greater things to lesser ones" (Augustine). It implies a radical assumption of responsibility for one's body and demands not repudiation of the body or sexuality, but their integration in one's personal life. Each of us is called to obey the command to be our own body, to express our sexuality according to the logic of the symbol and not that of the object. In particular, we need to remember that integrating *temporality* in love is essential: chastity is waiting, gradation, and duration. It refuses the fusionality of an "everything now" mentality and the logic of immediacy and consumerism. We can also see it as a way of resisting blind obedience to the sexual impulse, its impersonalization, the search for satisfaction at any cost, dissipation, and an excessive exaltation of sexuality. Chastity reminds us that love is also discipline, work, and effort and that it requires a process of purification if it is to become intelligent and respectful of the other person and his or her mystery, and thus truly attentive to the other's well-being. Rilke writes, "There is nothing more arduous than love—it is work, day after day. Young people are not at all prepared for the difficulty of love; convention has tried to turn this great and complex relationship into something simple and light, something that is within everyone's reach. But that isn't how it is. Love is difficult!" (Rilke 1979, 48–49).

Chastity, then, concerns each person. From a Christian perspective, it is not the unique responsibility of so-called consecrated celibates, but is an aspect of Christian life that should be taken seriously by every baptized person, whatever his or her life situation may be. Certainly, from a Christian point of view chastity is connected to one's faith in Christ and personal attachment to him; it is rooted in the decision to follow him and is an expression of love for him. In marriage just as in celibacy, chastity is respect for the mystery of one's own body and the bodies of others. It allows us to perceive the body as personal and expressive before grasping it as an object of desire. In fact, we are led to confess that the human body is a temple of the Holy Spirit and the dwelling place of God (1 Cor. 6:19), as well as the place where God is glorified (1 Cor. 6:20). Only great love for the Lord and faith in the Resurrection, together with human maturity characterized by adherence to reality and the ability to love, make it possible to live in celibacy for the sake of the kingdom of God. As Freud himself observed, human equilibrium can be essentially defined as the concrete ability to love and to work efficiently. These two capacities characterize the human maturity that is essential to full spiritual growth, not only in married life but also in celibate life.

Chastity implies a profound orientation of the heart and is therefore a journey, a battle that requires constant vigilance, and never a condition reached once and for all. St. Caesarius has the following to say: "Among all the battles Christians have to fight, the hardest are those for chastity: here one combats daily, and victory is rare." Victory is always a gift, an event of grace in which the energies of the Resurrection triumph, through faith, over human egocentric impulses. Christians find sustenance and direction for this struggle in the Eucharist, which reminds them that "the body is not meant for immorality but for the Lord, and the Lord for the body" (1 Cor. 6:13). There, as they examine their own lives before the body of the Lord given in love, they come to understand the relationship they should have with their own body and with the bodies of others. They also see themselves confirmed in their vocation to communion, love, and fellowship, and this calling leads them to make themselves a sign of God's love for humanity. As chastity creates in us a pure heart that is able to see reality and other people in God, it also makes us living reflections of God's love and power—the power with which "God raised the Lord and will also raise us" (1 Cor. 6:14).

31

OBEDIENCE

W e must obey God rather than any human authority" (Acts 5:29). The great biblical principle of *obedience* is profoundly *liberating*. From a biblical perspective, obedience is inseparable from freedom: only those who are free can obey, and it is only by obeying the gospel that one enters into the fullness of freedom. Bonhoeffer put it succinctly: "Obedience without freedom is slavery; freedom without obedience is anarchy" (Bonhoeffer 1969, 211–12). Before we look more closely at the Christian proprium of obedience, we should recall its anthropological basis. There is a fundamental form of obedience each of us is called to assume with regard to our past, our origins, our body, our family—in short, we are called to obey a series of situations, people, times, places, events, and conditions that have preceded us and given us our identity, and over which we have not had the slightest control or possibility to choose. The baggage already waiting for each of us at birth accompanies us along the path of our existence. Believers see this obedience as "creaturely" and recognize it as part of the *acceptance of limits* that defines their identity as created beings before their Creator. The acceptance of limits allows men and women to become human by resisting the temptation of totality—in other words, the temptation to make themselves equal to God. In the Genesis account of creation, this is the meaning of the prohibition against eating the fruit of the tree of knowledge of good and evil: human beings are human to the extent that they limit their ambition. The human relationship with God takes place within the domain of the *limited* and the *finite*. According to the Bible, obedience is to be understood in the context of this relationship—in other words, within the category of the *covenant*. This is the relationship with God that makes obedience to the law revealed to Moses on Sinai liberating and even joyful. If the law is a manifestation of the will of God, the partner who dictates the covenant, obedience to all of God's commands becomes the expression of the desire of the believer, who loves his or her God and finds joy in doing God's will. The formula used in Exodus 24:7 to indicate the people of Israel's acceptance of God's will as expressed in the law is significant: "All that the LORD has spoken, we will do, and we will listen." Here praxis, or putting the Word into practice, comes before listening to the Word, as if to suggest that the fundamental assent Israel offers God is more important than a specification of the contents of each single command. This text also means that it is only when we put the Word into practice—in other words, when we obey it concretely—that we truly understand it. This grounding of obedience within the covenant, a relationship in which the believer listens to his or her God, sets the tone for Christian obedience as well.

In the New Testament *listening*, intended in the sense of perception of God's will, is fully realized only when a person obeys God's will in faith and through his or her actions. The fulfillment of listening (*akouein/audire*) is obedience (*hypakouein/obaudire*)—that form of obedience that consists in believing. Paul speaks several times of the "obedience of faith," by which he means to say that faith takes the form of obedience, and that obedience reveals one's faith. The proprium of Christian obedience, however, is found in Christ's own obedience. The three most significant texts that speak of Christ's obedience (Rom. 5:19: "By the one man's obedience the many will be made righteous"; Phil. 2:8: "[Christ] humbled himself and became obedient to the point of death"; Heb. 5:8: "[Christ] learned obedience through what he suffered") form a synthesis of the life, mystery, and saving work of Jesus, describing Jesus's life and death as a form of obedience. At the center of Jesus's obedience is his filial relationship with the Father, and at the heart of his obedience is love for his Father and for his brothers and sisters, for humanity.

The fourth Gospel underscores Jesus's obedience by presenting him as a person who is totally dispossessed of himself and who, in all that he says, does, and is, continues to point to the Father who sent him. This loving obedience gives meaning to his living and dying, and makes even his death on the cross an act of freedom. This is where Christian obedience finds its place, its "measure" and its form: the form obedience takes in our lives is given by the Holy Spirit, who insists that we express our obedience creatively and responsibly, not legalistically. Yes, the criterion in Christian obedience is the Holy Spirit, who interiorizes the demands of the gospel in each of us and leads us to see them as expressions of God's will, so that we can then apply them to our lives to the point that they become expressions of our own will. In the light of this fundamental obedience, we can understand, accept, and carry out other acts of obedience, in response to requests in which we perceive a mediation of God's will. As we do so, we should always remember that everything should be governed by the gospel and submitted to the decisive criterion of the gospel. When forms of mediation of God's will (ecclesiastical authorities, theological doctrines, monastic rules, cultural rites, etc.) take the place of God and claim that obedience is due to them, they should be subjected to criticism and led back to obedience to the gospel, because "we must obey God rather than any human authority."

32
POVERTY

Any Christian discussion on the subject of poverty requires great delicacy. The topic is easy to manipulate: certain Gospel texts, if removed from their contexts, can be used to justify a form of severity that is radical and impracticable, and therefore unreal. At the other extreme, the current exaltation of the "market" has led some to go so far as to search for (and claim to find) a foundation for the capitalist system in the gospel. I want to recognize, on the one hand, the misleading character of the various forms of demonization of the "market," "enterprise," and so on that we sometimes encounter in ecclesial environments. I also want to recall the fact that the judgments made in ecclesial environments with regard to economic issues and situations are often inaccurate, totally incompatible with reality, based on archaic stereotypes that have little or nothing to do with today's economic situations, and therefore ideological or simply useless. What I would like to do here is reexamine the issue of poverty on the basis of the gospel and New Testament message, in order to bring forth some indications for our life today.

If we consider the gospel as a whole, we find that its message regarding poverty has meaning only if we refrain from isolating it, and instead contextualize it within the focal center of

Jesus's life and preaching: the announcement of the in-breaking of the kingdom of God, and the revelation that in Jesus God visits his people. The primacy of the kingdom, which becomes the primacy of Christ and of his call to discipleship, structures our relationships with all other human realities in such a way that they remain relative to the central reality of the kingdom. This is why the drawing near of the kingdom, present in the Messiah sent to the poor, makes the poor blessed (Lk. 6:20–26). They are proclaimed blessed not because they are poor, but because in the Messiah they are given the pledge of an end to their poverty: the kingdom that God will establish fully belongs to them. At the same time, as Jesus acknowledges the reality of a negative and multifaceted poverty that includes evil, illness, sin, and death—in summary, everything that damages the fullness of human life and from which men and women must be liberated—he asks for inner poverty, poverty in spirit (Matt. 5:3), which concerns not what we have but who we are. Poverty in spirit is the attitude of faith and humility that belongs to those who do not trust in themselves, their own possessions or their own strength, but in the Lord. The primacy of the kingdom drastically reduces the priority of wealth for Christians. Jesus asks his followers to be on their guard against wealth, which can take possession of the heart and become an idol ("mammon"), thereby taking the place of God and dehumanizing the person. Well before Jesus, Aristotle had already called the attitude of those who seek happiness by accumulating possessions "against nature": possessions or wealth can only be a means, not an end. Poverty has an anthropological dimension that we absolutely must incorporate into our lives, as part of our obedience to the calling we have received as created beings, namely, the calling to become who we are.

The savage criticism of wealth and the invective against the rich we find in the letter of James certainly do not exhaust the New Testament message regarding poverty and wealth, but they reveal a prophetic and critical stance that the church should maintain in every age, even if this leads to collisions between the church and secular authorities. In fact, one of the ways Jesus expresses the gospel requirement of poverty is in terms of freedom from power. "Not so with you" (Lk. 22:26) is his categorical command, which defines the church as a Eucharistic community that should be structured in a way that sets it apart from secular, worldly powers. Here poverty is placed in opposition to power. A Christian community, since it acts as a reminder of the values of the gospel, has a countercultural function, a responsibility to assume a critical position with regard to the dominant power. This capacity, however, is active only when the church defines authority not as power but as service. If we reduce poverty to a private virtue, we lose part of its evangelically critical potential. It is significant that when the late-medieval church failed to assume a critical position with regard to the economic evolution then taking place in society, it removed poverty from its canonical ideal of holiness. Not until Vatican II was there again an effort to speak of the church as "poor" and "of the poor," and not only "for the poor" or "with the poor." We are rediscovering the Christological foundation of poverty: "Christ, though he was rich, for your sakes became poor, so that by his poverty you might become rich" (2 Cor. 8:9). This Christological foundation makes it clear that poverty is a requirement of the gospel that is essential for all Christians, and not a suggestion reserved for some.

The gospel requirement of poverty, however, is not a law that specifies the forms poverty should take in different social circumstances. The New Testament itself presents many different forms of poverty: selling, sharing, or abandoning one's possessions, renunciation, collections for poor churches, and so on. The Christological foundation of poverty becomes Trinitarian if we realize that Christ is poor because he receives from the Father all that he has, says, and does, according to the fourth Gospel. This inter-Trinitarian relationship of mutual listening and receptivity between the Father and the Son becomes communication with humanity through the gift of the Spirit. It is the Spirit who awakens Christians' creativity in every age and guides them toward obedience to the eternal gospel in each new historical context.

The Christological and Trinitarian foundation of poverty should lead the church to examine itself regarding at least two aspects of its own poverty, which together represent a challenge Christianity will face in the coming years. First, the church's *missionary activity* should be poor—that is, it should adapt Jesus's extremely strict standards regarding the poverty of disciples sent on mission to today's missionary environments (see Lk. 9:1–6; 10:1–16). Only a missionary initiative that is itself poor can approach those who are poor without contradicting the gospel it announces, which is "the word of the cross." Christ made himself poor to the point of giving himself on the cross, and this giving is the fullest expression of his poverty. The church also needs to think of poverty not simply as a personal virtue but as a *dimension of community and ecclesial life*. This will only be possible if the church regains consciousness of its eschatological horizon, and if it allows this awareness to shape ecclesial institutions and influence the way the church situates itself in the world. Thinking of poverty as an ecclesial and community reality also means listening to the voices of the millions of poor who cry out to God for justice.

33
FASTING

n Western Christianity today we are observing a de facto elimination of the ecclesial practice of fasting. Although fasting was practiced by the people of Israel, reproposed by Christ, and incorporated into the great ecclesial tradition, it is less and less present today, and often our churches no longer request it. Yet if we want to discover the truth of who we are, the truth of our humanity, which, with grace, becomes Christian truth, we need to think, pray, share what we have, and recognize the evil that dwells in us—but we also need to practice the form of oral discipline that is fasting. Eating belongs to the category of desire, because it goes beyond the simple function of providing us with nourishment and takes on highly significant affective and symbolic connotations. As human beings we are nourished not only by food but also by the words and gestures we exchange with others, by relationships and love, and by everything else that gives meaning to the life food sustains and builds up in us. We also eat *together* with others, in an atmosphere of conversation and conviviality.

Eating, speaking, and kissing are all forms of oral expression, and since they are connected to the biological, communicative, and affective dimensions of human life, they involve the entire person who receives life through these dimensions. Fasting carries out the basic function of helping us identify what it is that we hunger for, what gives us life, and what nourishes us, so that we can set our different appetites in order in a way that allows what is truly central in our life to remain central. We would be deceiving ourselves profoundly if we thought that fasting, which has been practiced in many different forms and degrees in Christian tradition—total fasting, fasting from meat, a diet of vegetables or of bread and water—could be replaced by any other form of ascetic discipline. Eating is particularly significant because it is an infant's first way of relating to the external world. Infants are nourished by their mothers' milk, but as they are initially unable to distinguish their mother from food, they also seek nourishment in all that surrounds them. They "eat" and take in voices, odors, shapes, and faces, and through this process they gradually construct a personality, relationships, and an emotional life. This means that the symbolic value of fasting is connected to all of the external aspects that contribute to the construction of our identity. Other forms of asceticism cannot be considered "equivalents" to fasting, because they are associated with other symbolic values and are thus unable to carry out fasting's unique function. Different ascetic practices are not interchangeable!

When we fast, we learn to recognize and control our many appetites by first controlling our most basic and vital appetite, hunger. We learn to exercise discipline in our relationships with others, with external reality, and with God, relationships in which the temptation of voracity is always present. Fasting is a way of disciplining our need and educating our desire. Only an insipid and ignorant form of Christianity that thinks of itself more and more as social morality can dismiss fasting as essentially irrelevant, and can make the mistake of thinking that any resolution to go without something "extra" (and therefore not as vital as food and eating) can take the place of fasting. This is a docetic trend that makes the created reality of human beings only "apparent," and that forgets both the body's significance and "density" and the fact that the body is a temple of the Holy Spirit. Fasting is actually the way a Christian confesses faith in the Lord with his or her entire body. It is an antidote to our tendency to reduce the spiritual life to its intellectual dimension, or to confuse the spiritual with the psychological. Certainly, as there is always the risk of our turning fasting into an ascetic performance or an accomplishment deserving of a reward, the Christian tradition reminds us that our fasting should be hidden and governed by humility, and that it should have a precise objective—justice, the sharing of what we have, and love for God and our neighbor (Isa. 58:4–7; Matt. 6:1–18). This is the reason the Christian tradition has conducted a carefully balanced and judicious reflection on the subject of fasting: "Fasting is useless and even dangerous for those who are not familiar with its peculiarities and conditions" (John Chrysostom); "It is better to eat meat and drink wine and not to eat the flesh of one's brothers through slanderous words" (Abba Hyperechius); "If you fast regularly, do not be inflated with pride; if you think highly of yourself because of it, then you had better eat meat. It is better for a man to eat meat than to be inflated with pride and glorify himself " (Isidore the Elder).

We are indeed what we eat, and the believer does not live by bread alone, but above all by the Eucharistic Word and Bread and by the divine life they transmit. The personal and ecclesial practice of fasting is one of the ways we follow Jesus, who fasted (Matt. 4:2); it is an expression of our obedience to the Lord, who asked his disciples to pray and fast (Matt. 6:16–18; 9:15; Mk. 9:29); it is a confession of faith expressed with our body; and it is a pedagogical tool that teaches us to worship God with our entire being. (We should note that the verb "worship" or "adore" refers us to the mouth, *os-oris*, and therefore to the oral dimension of life.) Today, in a society in which consumerism has dulled our ability to distinguish true needs from false ones, in which fasting and dieting have become an industry, in which fasting is easily associated with Asian ascetic techniques, and in which Lent is sometimes equated with the Muslim Ramadan, Christians should remember the anthropological basis of fasting as well as its specifically Christian significance. Fasting is truly an essential aspect of faith because it leads us to the question, "As a Christian, what is it that gives you life?"

34
HOPE

n his *Commentary on the Psalms* (118.15.7), Hilary of Poitiers repeats a question that was being addressed to Christians by many of his contemporaries: "Christians, where is your hope?" Today, Christians and their churches should realize that this question is still being addressed directly to them. If it sometimes contains tones of self-sufficiency or skepticism, this matters little: Christians know that hope is their *responsibility*! They are called to give an answer to anyone who asks for a reason for their hope: ("Always be ready to make your defense to anyone who demands from you an accounting of the hope that is in you," 1 Pet. 3:15). Today this responsibility has become a crucial one. It is one of the critical challenges the church faces: is the church able to open up vistas of meaning? Does it know how to let its hope for the coming of the kingdom, which was the hope of Christ, be the source of its life? Does it know how to give hope and the possibility of a future to concrete, personal lives, and show that it is worth living and dying for Christ? Is the church able to call people to a life that is filled with beauty, happiness, and meaning because it is filled with hope, as was the life of Jesus of Nazareth? These questions cannot be avoided, today in particular when our cultural horizons seem to close us within the present, making it difficult for us to come up with long-term hopes that are capable of sustaining us over the course of our lifetime. In our "society of uncertainty" (insightfully described by Zygmunt Bauman 1999), in a moment of history in which we continue to talk about the "end" (of the century, the millennium, modernity, ideologies, the Christian world), in a time in which time is fragmented, and in which even the few hopes that manage to express themselves in society are irreparably short-term and fail to take root, because they are refuted as soon as they are set forth—in such a time, the question, What can we hope for? has become extremely urgent. It is striking to note how, in the church, the attention given to the beginning of the new millennium was accompanied by a distressing inability to open pathways toward the future. The church seems unable to show that there are concrete ways to live in hope and to work toward a meaningful future, and in particular, it does not seem to know how to offer hope or be present in a meaningful way to those for whom the future is on the immediate horizon—young adults.

It seems that the enemy of hope today is *indifference*, which we can trace to a sense of lack of meaning, or even a sense of the *irrelevance of meaning*. Even the emphasis in today's pastoral environments on charitable and volunteer activities has, in addition to many positive aspects, a tendency to limit the attention of Christians to the present, at times making it difficult for them to look beyond what needs to be done today to help those in need. Many of those who participate in charitable and volunteer work make only a short-term commitment that can be withdrawn at any time and that does not engage their future. It is in front of situations such as these that we should remember the question, "Christians, where is your hope?" The theological virtue of hope must be expressed in a visible, concrete, and lasting way in a concrete place; otherwise, it becomes illusion and rhetoric! An interesting passage of Augustine tells us that "only hope makes us Christians" (*City of God* 6.9.5). In other words, our experiences as Christians are not new or different in themselves, but hope leads us to invest our experiences, our relationships, and all of reality with a new and different meaning. Defining hope is not difficult; what is difficult is actually living in hope! Certainly, we can call hope an "active struggle against desperation" (Marcel 1967, 47) and "the capacity for intense activity not yet expended" (Fromm 1978, 19), but hope is above all what allows us to walk on the pathway of life, to be human— we cannot live if we do not hope! *Homo viator, spe erectus*: it is hope that keeps us on our feet and walking forward, and that makes us capable of facing the future.

Christians find their hope in Christ ("Christ Jesus our hope," 1 Tim. 1:1)—in other words, they find in Christ the ultimate meaning that illuminates all realities and relationships. In this sense, Christian hope is a powerful reservoir of spiritual energy, a dynamic element grounded in faith in Christ, who died and is risen from the dead. Christ's victory over death is the source of the believer's hope that evil and death, in all of the forms in which they appear in human life, will not have the last word. Christians share their hope with others through forgiveness, which conveys the message that no fault committed has the power to close the door to the future of a life. They also communicate their hope by living among others in a way that expresses their faith that God wills the *salvation of all people*, as the Paschal event makes clear (1 Tim. 2:4; 4:10; Titus 2:11). Most importantly, Christians communicate their hope by living according to the *logic of the Paschal event*. This is the "logic" that makes it possible for Christians to live in community with people they did not choose themselves, and it also makes them capable of loving even their enemies, those who are difficult to love, and those who express hostility toward them. It is Paschal logic that leads Christians to endure hardships, trials, and suffering with joy and serenity, and it is what guides them toward giving their lives—that is, toward martyrdom. If we want to see an authoritative narration of Christian hope in the church today, it is toward situations of martyrdom and persecution that we should look. There the hope of eternal life, of life in Christ beyond death, finds a mysterious, disquieting, yet extremely concrete and convincing narration. There Augustine's words become credible: "Now our life is hope; then it will be eternity" (*Commentary on the Psalms* 103.4.17).

35
FORGIVENESS

T he event at the heart of Christianity, the
revelation of God in Christ crucified, is interpreted
by Paul as an event that reveals God's love for human
beings even in their sin, and even when they make
themselves God's enemies (Rom. 5:8–11). It is an event
that reveals God's love and his free initiative, rather
than a juridical desire for compensation for the offense of human
sin. This means that the gift of the Son to humanity is also,
and at the same time, *forgiveness*, or remission of sins. Biblical
revelation expresses very clearly the fact that forgiveness is
unconditional. It is not preceded by repentance, as if repentance
were a necessary first step toward obtaining forgiveness. On
the contrary, forgiveness makes repentance possible and is
the source from which repentance flows. In the parable of the
prodigal son (Lk. 15:11–32) we learn that the son's change of
heart begins only when he realizes the depth of the faithful love
shown to him by his Father, who did not stop loving him during
his absence. What the son experiences as forgiveness is, in his
Father's eyes, nothing other than faithful love, love that is never
withdrawn. We will be able to understand forgiveness only if
we realize that it is tied to the freedom of loving and giving.
The word *forgiveness* itself suggests the *giving of something extra* that

takes place when we renounce a juridical relationship in favor of a relationship of grace.

We can see why forgiveness is central to Christian identity: God's statement (what God has accomplished in his Son Jesus Christ) has become a human imperative (what each individual Christian and the church are called to give witness to). It is not surprising, then, that the three critical steps in the formation of the church, as they are described in the Gospels, are marked by forgiveness of sins. The authority conferred upon Peter, the rock upon which the church is built, is essentially the power to forgive (Matt. 16:19). The Eucharist, which gives the entire ecclesial community its structure, is a powerful memorial of the event in which Christ poured out his blood "for the forgiveness of sins" (Matt. 26:28). The missionary responsibility entrusted to the disciples enables them to forgive sins (John 20:23). These events show us that "the church is a community of forgiven sinners who live because of the grace accorded to them through forgiveness, and who pass this grace on to others" (Ratzinger 1991, 107).

We find the idea of forgiveness in other cultural and religious environments, but in the Christian economy forgiveness is inseparably tied to the scandal and paradox of the cross—that is, to the Paschal event. The strength and weakness of the cross are reflected both in the omnipotence of forgiveness (everything can be forgiven) and in its extreme weakness (there is no guarantee that a person who has been forgiven will make a change of heart, nor is there any assurance that he or she will not use forgiveness as a pretext for continuing to behave wrongly). The message forgiveness conveys is that our relationship with the one who has offended us is more important than the offense. The one who has been offended places the wrong he or she has unjustly suffered in the *past*, where it will not affect the future of the relationship.

There is a fundamental asymmetry in Christian forgiveness: by forgiving the offender, the one who has been offended hands over to him or her, in a unilateral way, the only possibility to continue the relationship. For Christians, only faith in Christ and the gift of the Holy Spirit make such a gesture possible. Christ experienced this asymmetry on the cross: "The Just One whose resurrection we celebrate on Easter is the one who, in an asymmetrical way, restores reciprocity, answers hatred with love, and offers forgiveness to those who do not ask for it" (Jacques 1987, 335). It is the Spirit, breathed by the crucified and risen Christ upon the disciples (John 20:22–23), who enables them to forgive sins. *In the Christian economy, forgiveness is not ethical but eschatological.* It is a prophecy of the kingdom of God, a sign of the Spirit's action, a manifestation of the spiritual energies of the risen Christ, and a revelation of the love of God the Father. As a reflection of the triune love of God, forgiveness is a participation in Christ's victory over death. If the Resurrection "says" that death does not have the last word, forgiveness "says" that sin does not have the last word and is not the truth of who a person is. It reminds us that a person who sins is a human being, not a sin personified, and that he or she is much more than the sum of his or her actions, however negative those actions may be. In this sense, forgiveness is a sign of our humanity and a force that makes us more fully human.

Certainly, it is worth repeating that forgiveness is not a law, but rather a possibility that knows no limits (we should recall the command to forgive "seventy times seven" in Matt. 18:22) set before the faith and freedom of each person. Even less is forgiveness a law we can impose on others. It is possible only within the space of freedom. If forgiveness were not offered freely, it would not be a gesture of love and would not communicate to others the free initiative of God's actions.

36
LOVING OUR ENEMIES

All people love their friends, but only Christians love their enemies." It is significant that when Tertullian (*Ad Scapulam* 1.3) seeks to express the Christian "difference," he chooses to focus on love of one's enemies. Love for our enemies is a genuine summary of the gospel: if the entire law is summarized in the commandment to love God and our neighbor (Mk. 12:28–33; Rom. 13:8–10; Jas. 2:8), life according to the gospel finds its full realization in Jesus's words and actions, which reveal that love for one's enemies is the fulfillment of Christian praxis. Jesus said, "Love your enemies, do good to those who hate you" (Lk. 6:27; cf. Matt. 5:43–48; Lk. 6:28–29, 35), and his entire life—up until the moment he washed the feet of Judas, who had made himself his enemy; up until the cross, where he expressed his love for his own "to the end" (John 13:1); up until his prayer for his torturers as they were crucifying him (Lk. 23:33–34)—proclaims his unconditional love for all, even his enemies. Christians, who are called to have in themselves the thoughts, attitudes, and will of Christ (see Phil. 2:5), find themselves confronted with this requirement day after day.

Yet we cannot help asking, is it really possible to love our enemies, and to love them as they are displaying their hostility, opposition, hatred, and aversion? Is such a scandalous return of love for hatred humanly possible? We learn from experience that our fascination with the idea of total love for our enemies vanishes without a trace when we are faced with specific, concrete situations of hostility, and in such situations we find ourselves unable to act in a way that corresponds to our convictions. Perhaps this experience is already a first small step, and one that is humanly necessary, along the path toward loving our enemies.

In addition to this, the gospel leads each Christian to recognize him- or herself as an enemy loved by God and for whom Christ died. This fundamental experience of faith is the only possible departure point for the spiritual journey that leads us toward love for our enemies! Paul writes, "God proves his love for us in that while we were sinners and enemies Christ died for us" (Rom. 5:8–10). We must join to this experience of faith a step-by-step journey toward human maturity in which we learn to view alterity as positive, to meet others, to build relationships, and to grow in love.

In the Old Testament, the invitation made to the Israelites to love their neighbors as themselves is proposed as part of an itinerary: "I am the LORD. You shall not hate in your heart anyone of your kin; you shall reprove your neighbor, or you will incur guilt yourself. You shall not take vengeance or bear a grudge against any of your people, but you shall love your neighbor as yourself: I am the LORD" (Lev. 19:17–18). What is first asked is personal attachment in faith to the one who is the Lord. The Israelite is then called to avoid feelings of hatred (a negative attitude), to correct those who do wrong (a positive attitude) without seeking revenge (a negative attitude), and, in this way, to love his neighbor as himself (a positive attitude). Love is reached through a journey, and it requires practice.

Love is not spontaneous: it involves discipline, asceticism, and a struggle against the instinct of anger and the temptation of hatred. Through this combat we acquire the responsibility and courage that allow us to correct our brothers and sisters, criticizing in a constructive way the wrong done by others. Love for our enemies is not the same as complicity with those who sin! Rather, the freedom of those who know how to correct and reprove those who do wrong springs from deep faith and love for the Lord, and this faith and love are the necessary precondition for loving our enemies. Those who do not hold grudges or take revenge, but who correct their brothers and sisters, are also capable of forgiveness: and forgiveness is the mysterious maturity of faith and love that allows us, when we have been offended, to choose freely to renounce our own rights in a relationship with someone who has already trampled on our rights. Those who forgive sacrifice a juridical relationship in favor of a relationship of grace! When Jesus asks those who follow him to love their enemies, he also asks them to undertake a journey. We are called, first, to make an effort to go beyond the *lex talionis* ("an eye for an eye") in each new situation we face. We must then reach the point of not offering resistance to those who wrong us, countering evil with the extremely active passivity of nonviolence, and trusting in God, who is the one Lord and Judge of human hearts and actions. An enemy is our greatest teacher, because he or she unveils what is in our heart but does not emerge when we are on good terms with others. If we are convinced of this, we will find it possible to obey the words of our Lord, who asks us to turn the other cheek and to hand over even our cloak to the one who wants to take our tunic. For all of this to happen, prayer and intercession for our persecutors and adversaries are indispensable. The Gospels, which place this commandment next to the command to love our enemies ("Love your enemies and pray for those who persecute you," Matt. 5:44), remind us of this. Unless we carry others in prayer—and in a particular way others who make themselves our enemies, oppose us, act with hostility toward us and insult us—and unless we let prayer teach us to see others through God's eyes, in the mystery of their identity and vocation, we will never manage to love them! Yet it must be said clearly that loving our enemies requires deep faith, "intelligence of the heart," interior riches, and love for God, and not simply good intentions!

37
HUMILITY

Humility is a suspect virtue. The word is joined to a long legacy that has made it a personal virtue, the goal of the individual who seeks to become perfect. Humility is often seen as synonymous with a created being's self-annihilation in front of God, who is all, and his or her self-abasement in front of other people. Today, however, this is no longer felt to be an appropriate way of approaching God, who does not crush what is human but welcomes us in the fullness of our humanity. At times, humility is seen as a pose, an artificial attempt to downplay one's identity and worth. Psychologists understandably prefer the word "authenticity," whose meaning is actually quite close to the original meaning of the traditional term *humilitas*. For Nietzsche, humility is an aspect of the religious quest for consolation in the face of our own powerlessness. Not only is humility suspect; but in a certain sense it is also dangerous. It is dangerous to preach humility and make it a law, because we need to remember that such a message will be received in different ways by different people. Those with an inflated ego will probably not be affected in the least by anything said about humility, while those with a low self-image may respond in a way that is not psychologically healthy.

We should first ask ourselves, what is humility? The numerous definitions the Christian tradition has handed down to us guide us toward an understanding of humility as relative: relative, that is, to the diversity of individuals and to the different possible expressions of personal freedom. According to its most common definition, which is also the definition that best captures its unique character, humility is not exactly a virtue, but is rather the basis and motivation for all of the other virtues. "Humility is the mother, the root, the nurse, and the foundation of all the other virtues, and it is what holds them together," writes John Chrysostom; and in this context we can understand why Augustine sees "all of Christian discipline in humility alone" (*Sermon* 351.3.4). If this is the case, we need to free humility from the confines of subjectivism and devotionalism and remember that its source is Christ, who is *magister humilitatis* ("the teacher of humility"), in Augustine's words. Christ teaches humility by "teaching us to live" (Titus 2:12) and guiding us toward a realistic knowledge of ourselves. This is exactly what humility is: our courageous *acceptance of who we are in front of God*—in front of the God who revealed his own humility in the self-emptying of the Son, the *kenosis* of Christ that led to his death on the cross. Insofar as humility is authentic self-knowledge, it wounds our narcissism, because it leads us back to who we really are—that is, to our *humus*, our identity as created beings. This is how humility guides us along the path toward human maturity. This is genuine *humilitas*: "O man, realize that you are man; all of your humility consists in knowing yourself" (Augustine).

If we learn humility from the one who is "gentle and humble in heart" (Matt. 11:29), we will become the terrain upon which grace can develop and bear its fruit. When we recognize the limits that characterize us as created beings, our sinfulness, and, at the same time, the fact that we have received everything from God and are loved even in our limitations and negativity, humility becomes our joyful submission to God and our brothers and sisters in love and gratitude. Our humility depends on our love. "Where there is humility, there is also love," writes Augustine, and a contemporary philosopher expresses the same idea in his own terms: "Humility disposes and opens us to grace, but this grace is love alone, and not humility" (Jankélévitch 1970, 557). In this sense, humility is also an essential element of every form of community life. It is not by chance that in the New Testament, the apostles constantly invite the members of their communities to behave with humility: "Clothe yourselves with humility in your dealings with one another" (1 Pet. 5:5; see also Col. 3:12); "in humility regard others as better than yourselves" (Phil. 2:3); "do not be haughty, but associate with the lowly" (Rom. 12:16). Only humility makes possible the building up of a community, which always means bearing together each person's weakness and poverty. This is the only way we can combat and defeat pride, which is "the great sin" (see Ps. 19:13)—or perhaps more accurately, the great blindness that prevents us from seeing the truth about ourselves, others, and God. More than self-abasement, humility is an event that flows from the encounter between the God who has revealed himself in Christ and an individual created being. The humility of God revealed by Christ (cf. Phil. 2:8: "he humbled himself") becomes, through faith, our own humility.

Certainly, if we are to arrive at true humility—in other words, humility that is also truth—and if we are to learn how to adhere to reality by obeying God in gratitude, we sometimes need to experience humiliation. Humbling ourselves freely and with love is a difficult operation, and it is almost impossible to do with a pure intention. At times, humility can become an excuse to double our pride. This is why humility is not primarily a virtue to acquire, but rather an abasement to endure: *humility is above all humiliation*. This humiliation comes from others, especially those closest to us; it comes from life, which contradicts and defeats us; it comes from God, who is capable of humbling us and exalting us with his grace as no one else can. Humiliation is the place where we discover the truth of who we are and where we learn obedience, just as Christ "learned obedience through what he suffered" (Heb. 5:8)—namely, shame and disgrace (Heb. 12:2; 13:13). It is the event that takes us to the depths of our own abyss, where our heart is reduced to fragments: *cor contritum et humiliatum, Deus, non despicies* (Ps. 51:17: "A broken and contrite heart, O God, you will not despise"). After this experience, we can repeat with conviction the psalmist's words: "It was good for me that I was humbled, so that I might learn your statutes" (Ps. 119:71).

38

KNOWING OURSELVES

O ne of the most characteristic aspects of Christian spirituality has always been its attention to the dimension of interiority. Holiness does not consist in a series of performances, however generous, holy, or heroic—we encounter it on the level of being, and its objective is the conformity of the entire person to Christ. This means that in following Christ we are asked never to separate what is human from what is spiritual, and as we learn to know the Lord, we need to undertake the parallel journey that leads us toward self-knowledge. This is a theme that appears throughout the Christian tradition, which has not hesitated to adapt and rephrase in its own terms the inscription posted above the entrance of Apollo's temple at Delphi: "Know yourself." Origen and the Cappadocian fathers, Ambrose and Augustine, Gregory the Great, William of St. Thierry and Bernard, and the Carthusian and Victorine fathers have all explored in depth the meaning of self-knowledge, which is both an essential part of every person's journey toward becoming fully human ("The unexamined life is not worth living," Plato), and an essential process for every Christian who wants to begin his or her *sequela Christi* authentically. (The self-denial asked for by Christ must be undertaken freely and out of love, and this is only possible if we know ourselves.) Without an inner life, without the effort of learning to know ourselves, Christian spiritual life is impossible, and so is prayer!

There is a regrettable gulf today between the church and spiritual or inner life, and this is indicative of a crisis that is much more serious than any crisis evaluated in "numerical-quantitative" terms, because it tells us that the church is neglecting its responsibility to *initiate* Christians both to life and to life according to the Spirit. In addition to this, we cannot fail to note that the attention given today to the "I" and to the demands of subjectivity presents many ambiguities: cultural narcissism ("When wealth occupies a higher place than wisdom, when notoriety is more admired than dignity, and when success is more important than self-respect, this means that an entire culture overrates the *image*, and should be considered narcissistic," Lowen 1986, 7), spiritual pornography (the exhibition of the inner self, the disappearance of privacy that results in people's personal confessions or family problems being dished out to millions of television viewers), and the suppression of individuality by a technological culture that values workers who carry out preprogrammed tasks, which provokes the hypertrophy of the "I" in other existential environments. These trends should, on the one hand, make us cautious when we speak about what it means to know ourselves; on the other hand, they tell us how urgent a discussion on self-knowledge has become. Our human freedom depends on knowing ourselves! Those who know themselves are truly free because they are able to maintain well-balanced relationships with others and with reality, and because they are able to discover reasons to hope and trust in the future.

The process of learning to know ourselves begins when we respond to a *call*—the call that makes itself heard in us, for example, when we feel the need to spend some time alone to think, reflect, and "take a step back" from our daily life that threatens to numb us with its repetitiveness or overwhelm us with its frantic pace. We sense a call to make an *exodus* in the direction of our interiority, a journey toward the center of ourselves. We set out on this journey by *asking ourselves questions* (Who am I? Where am I coming from? Where am I going? What is the meaning of what I do? Who are other people for me? . . .), and by reflecting, *thinking*, and working through our experiences. Only this process of interiorization allows us to become subjects in our own lives, instead of letting our life "live itself." Certainly, this journey into our interiority, this descent into our heart, is laborious and painful. We usually refuse to undertake it for fear of what might emerge, what aspect of ourselves might come to light. Nietzsche spoke of the intense pain truth uses in revealing itself to a person. Knowing ourselves requires *attention* and *inner vigilance*, which is the ability to concentrate and to listen to *silence* that, with the help of *solitude*, helps us rediscover what is essential. With time we discover the meaning of *habitare secum*—we learn to inhabit our inner life, and we allow our inner truth to reveal itself in us. At this point, self-knowledge also means recognizing our limitations and what is negative and incomplete in us—in other words, the aspects of ourselves we usually tend to repress so that we will not have to confront them. Our knowledge of our poverty, together with our knowledge of God, can then become an experience of God's grace, mercy, forgiveness, and love. What we previously knew because we had been told about it now becomes a personal experience. For this to happen, we need to remember never to separate these two aspects of the spiritual itinerary: knowing ourselves and knowing God. Knowing ourselves without knowing God leads to desperation, and knowing God without knowing ourselves produces arrogance.

39

SOLITUDE

Solitude is part of our humanity: we are born alone, and we die alone. We are certainly "social beings" and are made "for relationships," but experience shows that only those who know how to live alone also know how to be fully themselves in their relationships. Also, every relationship, in order to remain a relationship and not degenerate into fusion or absorption, implies a certain element of solitude. Only those who are not afraid to descend into their own interiority also know how to handle the encounter with alterity. It is significant that many "modern" illnesses and problems that have to do with subjectivity also have the effect of undermining the quality of one's relationships. For instance, the inability to interiorize one's experiences and inhabit one's inner life leads to an incapacity to create and maintain solid, deep, and lasting relationships with others.

Of course, not all solitude is positive. There are forms of flight from others that are pathological, and there is above all the "negative solitude" of isolation, which implies shutting out others, rejecting one's desire for their presence, and resisting alterity. Yet between isolation, closure, and obstinate silence, on the one hand, and the distraction that results from talking constantly, needing to be in the physical presence of others, or rushing from one activity to the next, on the other hand, solitude is balance and harmony, strength and steadfastness. We can accept solitude if we have the courage to look ourselves in the face, if we recognize and accept the task we have been given to "become ourselves," and if we are humble enough to see that the full realization of our own uniqueness is something that no one else can do for us. We cannot avoid this responsibility by seeking refuge in the "mass," the anonymity of a crowd; nor can we hide behind an egotistic desire for solitude that leads us to turn away from others. Solitude guides us toward authentic self-knowledge, and it requires a great deal of courage.

Solitude is *essential in every relationship*: it is what allows a relationship to be a relationship, and it is within our relationships that we can best understand solitude. Our ability to love is proportional to our ability to accept solitude. If solitude is present in love, this is perhaps one of the great signs of love's authenticity. Simone Weil writes, "Preserve your solitude. If the day ever arrives when you are offered a true affection, *there will be no contrast between interior solitude and friendship*; in fact, this will be the infallible sign of friendship" (Weil 1962, 73). Solitude is the crucible of love: every great human and spiritual achievement emerges from solitude. In fact, solitude itself becomes the beatitude of those who know how to inhabit it. As Marie-Madeleine Davy writes, echoing the medieval expression *beata solitudo, sola beatitudo*: "Solitude is only difficult for those who do not thirst for their inmost selves and, as a result, are unaware that they have an inner self; it is supreme happiness to those who have tasted this intimacy" (Davy 1966, 55–56). Solitude, which we fear because it reminds us of the radical solitude of death, is in reality always *solitudo pluralis*, plural solitude. It is the space in which we seek the unification of our heart and communion with others; it is a way of making the other present in his or her absence; it is where our relationships, which tend to become insignificant when we are constantly in the company of others, are purified. For Christians, solitude is a space for communion with the Lord, who asked his disciples to follow him wherever he went—we should remember how much of Jesus's life was spent in solitude! Jesus who goes into the desert and struggles against the Tempter; Jesus who prays in deserted places, who seeks solitude in order to be close to his Father and discern his will. Certainly, Christians are called to fill their solitude, as Jesus did, with prayer and spiritual combat; they are called to discern the will of God in solitude and seek his face. Commenting on John 5:13, which reads, "The man who had been healed did not know who it was [who had healed him], for Jesus had disappeared in the crowd that was there," Augustine writes, "It is difficult to see Christ in the midst of a crowd; we need solitude. In solitude, if the soul is attentive, God lets himself be seen. Crowds are chaotic; to see God, you need silence." The Christ in whom we say we believe and whom we say we love makes himself present to us in the Holy Spirit, dwelling in us and making his home in us. Solitude is the space we lend to the discernment of this presence and to the celebration of the liturgy of the heart.

Christ, who experienced the solitude of betrayal, the departure of his disciples and friends, the rejection of his people, and even abandonment by God, also shows us how to endure solitude when it is imposed on us, loneliness, "negative" solitude. The One who, on the cross, experienced both total intimacy with God and abandonment by God, reminds us that the cross is a mystery of solitude and communion, a mystery of love.

40

COMMUNICATION

The quality of our life is determined by the quality of our relationships, which form the substance of our life. The quality of our relationships depends on the quality of our communication, at each of its levels: with ourselves, at an interpersonal, social, or political level, and so on. Christians find the model for their communication at a theological level, in God's communication of himself to humanity in Christ. Clearly, the problem of communication in the church cannot be reduced to the question of new technology and the need to take advantage of the opportunities it offers to reach a wider audience more effectively. If we recall that according to biblical revelation, the Holy Spirit is God's free will to communicate and enter into communion with men and women, we will understand that Christian communication can be truly sacramental—that is, it can convey something of the Trinitarian reality that gives the church its foundation and reason for existing, and toward which the church refers us— only if it invokes and lets itself be shaped by the Spirit's action. Christian communication should also seek to conform itself to the image of Christ, who, on the cross, "brings humanity back to a God who is not truly God except insofar as he is Communication itself" (Gustave Martelet).

This dimension of communication as revelation is joined to communication's anthropological dimension. In human terms, communication means above all "giving," making public what is ours and sharing it with others, and at the same time preparing ourselves to receive something from others. It is not a one-way process but a circular, reciprocal, and interactive movement in which the partners involved exchange signs and messages in the hope of reaching mutual understanding and agreement. This exchange never leaves unchanged those who take part in it: our identity is shaped *during* communication. Since we are communicative beings, no aspect of human behavior is exempt from this law! "With or without action, words or silence always have a communicative nature" (Watzlawick 1971, 42). It is clear that this is true not only for individuals but also for all human groups, and therefore for the church. One of the ways we can evaluate the church's faithfulness to the gospel is by looking at the quality of its relationships: the relationships that exist within the church, the relationships one Christian denomination establishes with another, the way the church approaches those who do not believe in God and those who belong to other religious traditions, the way it defines its presence in the world, its relationships with secular institutions, and so on. It is here that the church runs the risk of changing the *gospel*, the good news of God's communication to humanity, into *bad communication*. This happens when *parrhesia*, the evangelical boldness of Christ's disciples, gives way to the timidity and subservience of officials in an ecclesiastical institution; when authority, instead of remaining at the service of communion, degenerates into an arrogant display of power; when the ecclesial community plays favorites, privileging some and marginalizing others; when censorship, duplicity, hypocrisy, and half-truths create that climate of fear that is a direct contradiction of the evangelical freedom inspired by the Spirit; when dialogue is shunned rather than pursued, and so on. It is only when the Christian community makes itself an environment where authentic freedom is possible that it also becomes a space for discussion, dialogue, and communication among brothers and sisters!

Community life, which is the face of the Christian community and the fundamental form of testimony the church offers humanity, depends on communication. Communication is an art, not a technique, and it is an art that demands humility. It is not an overflowing fullness, an expression of an "extra" or a "too much"; rather, it arises from an emptiness, an awareness of a lack, a need. When we communicate, we express our need for others, we acknowledge that we depend on them and owe our life to them, and we confess that the gift of God, the *munus* from which our communication arises, precedes us. The Word of God that is communicated to us, and in which God gives himself to us in Christ, is the true beginning of Christian communication, a form of communication in which we are already immersed before we become aware of our participation and accept this participation as our responsibility. Those who know how to communicate are those who recognize their own ontological poverty as the truth of who they are. And those who know that they are poor are also able to pray, to communicate with God and respond to the gift of his Word, because they know how to listen and receive. It is on the foundation of this poverty that community, life together with others, can be built up: community life is always the fruit of bearing together each member's poverty and weakness, rather than the sum of the strength of all. The Christian community is a fruit of the Spirit, a sign of God's communication to men and women, a sacrament of the gift that is the Word of God, and a loving response to God, who first loved us. God, "who is in himself triune communion, creates communion with and among human beings by communicating his life to them, and asks that this life be communicated in turn to each brother and sister until it reaches all of creation" (Mancini 1991, 114).

41

COMMUNION

n Christian revelation, communion is first of all a theological reality. God in his own being is communion, the Spirit is the Spirit of communion, and Christ is a corporate person, the head of the body that is the church. Communion is the divine life of the Trinity, a life of mutual *listening*, *dialogue*, and *giving* among the divine persons. Since it is a fundamental aspect of the divine life, communion is also essential to the church: if the face the church presents to the world is not a face of communion, the church is reduced to a sociological organization and is no longer the church of God. The church is called to be a place where all cultural, social, political, and ethnic barriers and forms of discrimination are overcome. As a place of reconciled diversity, where differences are brought together in communion, the church is not only a reflection of the dynamic communion that unites the persons of the Trinity, but also an icon of reconciled humanity, an image of the redeemed cosmos, and a prophecy of the kingdom. And this is exactly what every Eucharist, as the heart of communion, should make manifest. Communion is the criterion that reveals whether the church is obedient to the vocation it has received from God, and whether it is carrying out its testimony and mission in the world.

As the depth of the divine life, communion is shared with humanity by God, who impoverishes, empties, and humbles himself out of love, and in so doing expresses his desire for communion with men and women. "God so loved the world that he gave his only Son, so that everyone who believes in him may . . . have eternal life" (John 3:16); "Since, therefore, the children *share* flesh and blood, he himself likewise *shared the same things*" (Heb. 2:14). The wellspring of communion is love, and it takes place when we exchange a higher place for a lower one, just as the One who was in the form of God emptied himself, taking human form and sharing the human condition to the point of death, "even death on a cross" (Phil. 2:8). In summary, the *form* and *foundation* of Christian communion is the cross, the mystery and passion of love. If we say this, we also acknowledge that communion within the church, among the churches, and between the church and all people is a gift of God! It is not programmable or achievable as the objective of a strategy of ecclesiastical politics, but must be welcomed as grace. We can prepare ourselves to receive the gift of communion through our radical obedience to the gospel and by listening to others: those with whom we live, Christians of other denominations, those who belong to other religions and cultures, and those who do not believe in God.

We should remember in this context that Christian communion, which descends from the Trinity, is formed by the cross, and is constantly revitalized by the Holy Spirit, demands that the church and each Christian reject both every evasion of responsibility ("Who is my neighbor?," Lk. 10:29) and every affirmation of self-sufficiency ("I have no need of you," 1 Cor. 12:21). At the same time, communion within the church cannot be grounded solely in a horizontal principle of attentiveness to the other or need of the other. If a church centers all of its attention on "the other," it faces the risk of becoming an affective community closed within the emotional gratification of an exclusive "I-you" relationship. Or it may lapse into rivalry and confrontation, adopting an "I against the other" stance and a missionary initiative that becomes imposition, and taking on the appearance of a sect that is aggressive toward the world. As yet another possibility, it may define itself as a source of charitable aid, a benefactor, or a philanthropic organization. In the first case communion atrophies and becomes sterile, in the second it is misunderstood and betrayed, and in the third it is reduced to charitable activity.

"The other" is not enough: we also need "the Third" and his transcendence. It needs to be clear that from a Christian perspective, the "other" always refers us to a Third who is the Lord, the Creator of all people, and the One who has formed each man and woman in his own image. It is the Word of God—the Word that purifies our words, gives our communication its form, and presides over our relationships—that creates *koinonia*, communion, and not our own words. Karl Barth writes, "The Church is the continually renewed communion of men and women who listen to and give witness to the Word of God." The Word of God summons and assembles all believers and binds them together in one body, and this dynamic action of the Word is the wellspring from which the church and the ecclesial communion draw their vitality. It is this communion that the sacramental signs of baptism and the Eucharist also seek to build up, because "in the one Spirit we were all baptized into one body" (1 Cor. 12:13), and "Because there is one bread, we who are many are one body, for we all partake of the one bread" (1 Cor. 10:17).

Christians truly are *communicantes in Unum*, in the one God, the Father, through the one Lord, Jesus Christ, and the one Spirit (see Eph. 4:4–6). In their communion with the One who is the source of all holiness, Christians, who already live in *solidarity with sinners*, can also take part in the *communio sanctorum*, communion with the saints in heaven, who already live forever in God. Only then is the church understood in the fullness of its mystery as communion.

42

ILLNESS

One of the facts that strikes readers of the Gospels is the number of people with physical or mental illnesses ("unclean spirits") Jesus met during his historical ministry. We can imagine that his encounters with these men and women disfigured by suffering must have left their mark on Jesus's own humanity, in terms of his compassion and attentiveness to those in need. Jesus describes his own mission with the words, "Those who are well have no need of a physician, but those who are sick; I have come to call not the righteous but sinners" (Mk. 2:17). These words have a theological dimension—Jesus's healings show the gospel "in action" and are revelations of the kingdom of God and a prophecy of the time when "no one will say, 'I am sick'" (Isa. 33:24).

How does illness appear in the light of Scripture? It is essentially a reality in which the person who is ill is called to listen again, to reflect, and to come to a new understanding of his or her condition and of history itself. Illness is a new point of view from which to look at reality. We see this in the book of Job, a classic example of the experience of illness in Scripture. Illness "unveils" our view of reality by laying it bare, stripping it of all embellishments and mystifications, revealing it in its rawness, and through this process leading it back to truth. Illness reminds us that we have no power over life, that life is not directly available to us, and that suffering is the fundamental question life places before us.

Certainly, the ways we respond to illness are numerous, extremely varied, and impossible to foresee: we may experience dejection, rebellion, denial, or bitterness, but other possible outcomes of illness are simplification, rediscovery of what is essential in life, refinement, and purification. In our illness we are called to accept responsibility for "assigning a meaning" to our suffering. Illness does not bring with it a meaning that has already been given; on the contrary, in many respects it destroys the meaning and purpose a person had attributed to his or her life. This is also true for the Christian, who "knows no path that bypasses pain, but a path— together with God—that passes through it. Darkness is not the absence of God but his concealment, in which we, by following him, search for him and find him once again" (Schuchardt 1990, 4).

Perhaps the most serious human and spiritual issue that is emerging today regarding illness is its reduction to a technical problem. This issue arises when illness is considered from a purely clinical point of view, and when the question of meaning is removed from the picture. The biblical teaching that sought to establish a connection between illness and sin (we find this idea throughout the ancient Near East—it should be ascribed to shared cultural practices rather than to revelation) addressed the question of meaning by placing illness in a context in which it could be "read," understood, accepted, personalized, and incorporated into a network of social relationships. What we are seeing today, as one of the consequences of the anesthetization of pain, is a sort of repression of illness: the individual has become a formidable "consumer of anesthesia" (Illich 1977, 150). This "technical" vision of illness makes it easy for us to forget that it is *the entire person who suffers* an illness: he or she cannot be reduced to a suffering limb or organ in an approach that limits itself to localizing the illness, thus decontextualizing and dehumanizing it by removing it from its biographical context. The patient—and this should be remembered by those who care for the ill or accompany them spiritually—is first of all *a person*. We can understand, then, why any "Christian spirituality of illness" is limiting from the outset.

> We do not need a spiritual pharmacy; we need wholesome, everyday food. We do not ask for a hospital chapel, we ask for the church. We need nothing other than an ecclesial spirituality. We do not ask anyone to open a new school of spirituality for us, in which all of life's problems are examined and adapted to the situation of those who are familiar with Koch's bacteria or Pott's disease, and in which everything is seen through the lens of illness and surrounded by hospital smells. We ask that people stop speaking to us and treating us as "sick people" as if they did not want to know anything else about us; before being people who are ill, we are men and women and children of God. (Quoted in Lochet 1950, 63–64)

This statement was made a number of years ago by a Christian organization for the sick. When Christians face illness, they find themselves called to confront the unknowns each person encounters in illness, to go through the different stages that accompany the onset and evolution of their condition (we might recall the phases identified by the doctor Elisabeth Kübler-Ross: shock, denial, anger, bargaining, depression, acceptance, peace), to deal with reactions they may not have expected (desperation or aggression, resignation or revolt), and to reconcile their new situation with their faith. They can certainly find help and comfort in prayer and faith, but they may also find that their faith, as well as the image of God they had previously known, undergoes a radical crisis. As their body deteriorates, their image of the God who is the Creator of the human body may fall to pieces.

Those who offer their companionship to a person who is ill have no recipes to give him or her, nor can they make the ill person's bedside the pulpit for a sermon or a theological treatise. No error would be more damaging than that of approaching the patient with the attitude of someone who knows exactly what he or she should do—this would immediately become a form of power that would have the effect not only of making the patient a victim but also of laying blame on him or her. The only way the companion can offer assistance is by being present, sharing the weakness and powerlessness of the person who is ill, and accepting the terms of the relationship he or she establishes. It is the patient who is the companion's instructor, and not vice versa. Jesus identifies with those who are ill, and not with those who visit or care for them: "I was sick and you took care of me" (Matt. 25:36). In the church as well, therefore, those who are ill should not be seen simply as people who need assistance; they should also be considered bearers of life's teachings. They should be listened to and learned from in their situations of weakness.

43

OLD AGE

can identify four reasons why old age seems bleak: first, it makes activity difficult; second, it weakens the body; third, it denies us almost every form of pleasure; fourth, it is not far from death." To this opinion of Cicero (*De senectute*) we can add another reason why old age is difficult today. The technological age has rendered obsolete the adage that linked old age with wisdom, and that saw the older adult as the guardian of a memory and an experience that made him or her a fundamental member of the social group. The "wisdom of old age" appears to have become a relic belonging to the distant past, or else to a past that, in cultures not yet touched by computer technology, is still present, but these cultures often seem more remote to us than our own distant past. In the context of a society that exalts productivity, efficiency, and utility, older adults find themselves marginalized and made superfluous and useless, and they themselves often feel that they are a burden to their family and society. In such a social context, old age becomes a difficult transition from a condition in which one is defined by one's work or social role to a sort of dead zone of pure negativity, "retirement," a limbo in which one is defined by who one no longer is and what one no longer does.

Any discussion on the subject of old age is in reality a plural discussion that needs to take into account each person's experience and his or her condition of physical and mental health; still, old age is always a time when life can be lived fully. It is a distinctive phase of an existential journey, and not merely death's waiting room. "Old age offers itself to men and women as an extraordinary possibility to see life not as a duty, but as grace" (Barth). Not everyone is given the chance to experience this stage of life—Jesus himself did not experience old age. One's later years are therefore a gift that can be accepted in freedom and with gratitude. As we grow older we become more attentive to others, we see relationships as increasingly important, and we appreciate each gesture of attention and friendship. Old age is also our great opportunity to look back over our life and find in it a meaning that unifies all that we have experienced. If we find ourselves able to say "thank you" for the past and "yes" to the future, we have performed a spiritual operation that is an essential step in preparing ourselves for our meeting with death: the integration of our life, reconciliation with our past.

Old age is a time for *anamnesis*, remembering, and also for *storytelling*. We feel the need to tell others about our life, so that, when our stories are welcomed and respected by those who listen to us, we can reaffirm our life's worth. By telling our own story, we can also communicate to others an experience of faith. Psalm 71, the "prayer of an old person," is a moving example of such a personal account of faith in old age. Despite the physical and mental deterioration that are part of the process of aging, the loss of strength, and the fact that we have fewer possibilities, we also find that we have the possibility to face in a more direct way the questions life places before us, without the evasions and illusions our many activities may have allowed us to entertain when we were younger. What is my worth? What meaning does life have? Why should I die? What is the meaning of the suffering and losses life is filled with? We can also address the religious question, the question of faith, with greater awareness and in greater depth. "When he was younger, the individual could still imagine that he was the one who went to meet his Lord. Old age should become his opportunity to discover that it is the Lord who comes to meet him and take in hand his destiny" (Barth, quoted in *Oh! Vieillir* 1992, 37).

Every phase of life has its *proprium*, its own specific character. Accepting old age fully will allow us to experience these years not as a time of regret or nostalgia but as an opportunity to *interiorize* what we have lived and to *return to what is essential*. This is part of the process of making peace with what we have lost that makes old age resemble a movement of kenosis or self-emptying. "What youth finds outside of itself, those who have reached the midpoint of life must find in their interiority" (Jung, quoted in Zumkeller 1994, 166). Here the fruitfulness that is possible in old age is revealed (see Ps. 92:14, "In old age they still produce fruit, they are always green and full of sap"), a fruitfulness that manifests itself in affection and gentleness, graciousness and serenity. Our later years are a time in which we can find our worth in who we are and not in what we do. Clearly, this does not depend on us alone; it depends to a great extent on those who are close to us, and it also depends on society, which can accompany us in our task of experiencing our later years as a fulfillment, and not as an interruption or an end.

Old age is a moment of truth that reveals that life is made up of losses and built on our acceptance of our limitations and poverty, our weaknesses and what is negative in us. By placing us in a situation of extreme poverty, old age makes us capable of perceiving the truth of who we are, that truth that goes beyond every exterior frill. Perhaps it is not by chance that for Luke, the Gospel opens with two elderly figures, Simeon and Anna, who recognize and point to Jesus as the Messiah. Older adults indicate a direction to follow and communicate their wisdom. With their peaceful acceptance of their age, before God and others, they are a sign of hope and an example of responsibility.

44

DEATH AND FAITH

The modern world has managed to debase the thing that is perhaps more difficult to debase than anything else, because it has a singular dignity: death" (Péguy, quoted in Adorno 1994, 127). This observation by Charles Péguy (1907) gave Theodor W. Adorno matter for reflection in his *Minima Moralia*. It gives us reason to reflect as well, we in the West who, a century later, see death repressed and at the same time flamboyantly exhibited, made obscene—in other words, banished from the land of the living, estranged from the world of social relationships—and at the same time turned into a spectacle and mercilessly exposed, as if in a media-officiated ritual of mass exorcism. A narcissistic society attempts to repress everything that reminds it of its limits, and in particular the event of death, which has the power to annihilate every human delusion of omnipotence. Yet in carrying out this anesthetic operation we forget that we are depriving ourselves of the reality that, more than any other, helps us understand ourselves, because it places life's "big questions" in front of us; the enigma that, in its irreducibility, can become a revelation, open up glimpses of meaning for our life, and above all, bring us out of the banality and mediocrity in which we often enclose ourselves. "When a person wants to understand himself, he must question himself about death" (Jüngel 1972, 21)—we should open ourselves to the scandalous power of the question death asks and is. By forgetting death or trying to conceal it, we contribute to the dehumanization of a culture and a society. How can we forget that it was when the Buddha saw a dead person and became aware of the reality of death (he had already become aware of the reality of illness and old age) that his initiation into the way of illumination began? As a young prince, the Buddha had always lived in royal palaces where, under his father's protection, he had been prevented from seeing the world's evil, but he found it necessary to break through the barrier that held him back from a direct encounter with the reality of the human condition.

Memento mori, the remembrance of death, is as relevant now as it has ever been! Christians, who know that the event of the death and resurrection of their Lord is at the heart of their faith, have the responsibility and *diakonia* of keeping *memoria mortis* alive in the world—not because they are cynical, have morbid tastes, or hold life in contempt, but in order to give life weight and significance. Only those who have a reason to die also have reasons to live! And only those who learn to lose, to accept the limitations of their existence, know how to accept death as a friend. The death of Christ teaches us how to die and how to live. In the Gospels Christ's death is not presented as a fact, a destiny passively endured, but rather as an act, the culminating event of a life. It is a death brought to life by love—God's love for humanity, the divine passion of love that becomes a passion of suffering in the Son's death for love. The way we experience death is connected to our experience of the death of the people we love—with their death, something in us also dies.

And if love is what gives life its meaning, it also leads us to the point of considering the loss of our life for someone we love an "obvious and logical" consequence of our love. We understand something about death, and suffer the consequences of death, to the extent that we love, but death is also capable of bringing our loves to an end, cutting them short from one moment to the next. We see death as more foreign and alienating than anything else, yet it is also what is most truly and originally ours, so much so that, in today's hospitals, the denial of death to those who are on the point of death is simply inhuman. Today, as Norbert Elias has noted, people die much more hygienically, but also much more alone, than they did in the past (Elias 1985, 104).

Christians, who place their faith not in immortality but in resurrection from death, know that their faith does not sidestep the grief of death but passes through it. They also know that God has taken upon himself the dramatic separation of death, and that death is not only an end but also a fulfillment. We can learn to make death an "act" in prayer, because prayer means giving time to God, and time is life. It is above all in prayer that death, our "enemy," can be experienced as life for God and with God, and can thus become our "sister." There is a wisdom that comes from "counting our days" (see Ps. 90:12)—in other words, accepting with serenity the limited number of days we are given in which to live, the dimension of temporality, and death. We can arrive at this peaceful acceptance by founding our lives on our faith in God, who called us to life and, in the same way, calls us to himself through death: "You turn humans back to dust, saying, 'Return, sons of Adam!'" (Ps. 90:3).

Christian faith is also a great battle against death, and above all against the fear of death that makes men and women "subject to slavery all their life" (Heb. 2:15). This battle against death is not an act of repression; it is a battle because death still shows the face of an enemy and an antagonist, and it is a battle in Christ, because many of the strategies we use in an attempt to escape the anxiety of death follow the logic of idolatry and sin. We are sustained in this battle by our faith that it is not death that will have the last word, but God himself and his love, the love that leads us through death to eternal life.

45
EPILOGUE: JOY

As believers in the good news of the gospel, Christians respond with joy to the salvation event accomplished by Jesus Christ. Joy is inseparable from Christian faith—for those who believe, it is not a possibility but a responsibility. The responsibility of joy descends from the Paschal event, in which God raised Jesus Christ and revealed to humanity the hope in the Resurrection. The entire gospel unfolds between the announcement of the great joy of the Savior's birth in Bethlehem (see Lk. 2:10–11) and the explosion of joy at dawn on the first day after the sabbath, the day of the Resurrection (see Matt. 28:8).

If we want to understand what it means to say that Christian life is joyful, we should ask ourselves what joy is in human experience. We may not manage to define it perfectly, but each of us has experienced joy. It is like a peak moment in our life, a sensation of fullness in which life seems positive, meaningful, and worthy of being lived. With Hans-Georg Gadamer we can call joy a revelation: "Joy is not simply a condition or feeling; it is a sort of revelation of the world. Joy reveals itself in our discovery that we are satisfied." In the experience of joy, our daily life undergoes a kind of transfiguration. The world gives itself to us, and we enter into joyful gratitude: "The only relationship between consciousness and happiness is gratitude" (Adorno 1994, 127). We are grateful because we are joyful. Joy is the experience of meaningfulness that opens the door to our future by giving us hope. It implies a relationship with time: there is the joy of waiting (for the arrival of someone we love, for a birth, etc.), the joy of someone's presence, and the joy of remembering (or, if we prefer, the memory of joy—as we remember, we relive the joy we have experienced in the past). This is especially evident during moments of *celebration*, when we experience the *joy of being together*—when does a celebration start, and when does it end? This is not easy to say, because it already exists in the joy of those who prepare it and wait for it to begin, and it continues to exist in the joy of those who remember it.

Joy is also connected to meeting others and to our positive experience of their presence. The words of greeting used by many cultures are significant: the Greek *chaire* (literally, "rejoice") wishes the other person joy at the moment of meeting, and the Hebrew *shalom* (and related terms in other Semitic languages) also wishes the other person a situation in which he or she might experience joy. We can say, in summary, that joy is an experience that embraces our entire existence and that makes itself felt with force in moments of love (the joy of friendship and love) and at times of celebration. (Sharing a meal together is a celebration par excellence of the joy of living, and of living together.)

We cannot fail to see that these dimensions of joy take on their full meaning in Christ, during the celebration of the Eucharist. It is "with joy" that we give thanks ("Give thanks to the Father with joy," see Col. 1:12), and the Eucharist is the joy of remembering the Paschal event, which we relive in the present, and the joy of waiting for its eschatological fulfillment, when the Lord comes in glory. It is also the joy, expressed in particular through the "holy kiss," of the communion that the presence of Christ creates among those gathered together: "Seeing everyone together at the Eucharist is a source of overwhelming joy" (Jerome). This joy "in Christ" is a joy that is extremely human—its physical dimension is never excluded, we express it in our human relationships, and it culminates in the Eucharistic meal, where the celebratory symbol becomes, in Christ, a prophecy of the eschatological banquet. The eschatological dimension of Christian joy also takes the form of "joy in affliction" (2 Cor. 7:4; Col. 1:24)—in other words, joy that does not disappear even in situations of suffering and contradiction.

This does not mean, of course, that as Christians we no longer experience moments of sadness or pain that make joy temporarily impossible. These moments exist, but Christian joy continues to dwell in our inmost depths as part of our life hidden in God. It is the indescribable and glorious joy (1 Pet. 1:8–9) of those who love Christ and already live with him in the secrecy of faith. It is the joy no one can take away from us, because no one can prevent a Christian from loving the Lord and his or her brothers and sisters even in situations of extreme suffering—the martyrs are there to remind us of this. Christian joy costs us a great deal because it means accepting our condition of temporality and mortality, but it allows us to make our inevitable descent toward death an ascent toward the Father. In our hope-filled journey toward our Lord, we look forward with joy to meeting the One whose face we have sought with longing during the days of our existence. This is why, in the New Testament, joy is an apostolic command: "Rejoice in the

Lord always; again I will say, Rejoice!" (Phil. 4:4). We can experience joy now, but there is also the fullness of joy that is to come,
the joy of meeting the Lord face to face. If joy is our responsibility
as Christians, we need to dedicate ourselves to practicing it—first,
because this will help us defeat the *spiritus tristitiae* ("spirit of melancholy") that always threatens us, and second, because we cannot
deprive the world of our testimony of the joy whose source is faith.
The joy of those who believe is what tells the world about the glory
of God! This is what the world asks: "Let the Lord show his glory;
and you, believers, let us see your joy!" (Isa. 66:5).

GLOSSARY

alterity: otherness

dialogical relationship: a relationship consisting of conversation, or dialogue, with another

ecclesial: of the church

hermeneutic: *adjective*: explanatory or interpretive; *noun*: explanation or interpretation

praxis: putting a concept into practice

polis: the state or government (a word related to politics)

proprium: the specific character of something

sapiential: oriented toward wisdom (rather than toward intellect)

telos: the ultimate goal or end

REFERENCES

Adorno, T. W. *Minima Moralia*. Turin: Einaudi, 1994.

Barth, K. in *Oh! Vieillir*. Le Mont sur Lausanne: Overture, 1992.

Bauman, Z. *La società dell'incertezza*. Bologna: Il Mulino, 1999.

Bloy, L. *La Femme Pauvre*. Mercure de France, 1956.

Bonhoeffer, D. *Etica*. Milan: Bompiani, 1969. (In English: *Ethics*. New York: Touchstone, 1995.)

———. *La vita comune*. Brescia, Queriniana, 1969. (In English: *Life Together*. New York: HarperOne, 2009.)

———. *Résistance et soumission*. Geneva: Labor et Fides, 1973.

Bunge, G. *Akedia: Il male oscuro*. Bose: Qiqajon, 1999.

Campo, C. *Gli imperdonabili*. Milan: Adelphi, 1987.

Catechismo della Chiesa Cattolica. Vatican City: Libreria Editrice Vaticana, 1992. (In English: *Catechism of the Catholic Church*. New York: Catholic Book Publishing Co., 1994.)

Chardin, T. de. *Le milieu divin*. Paris: Seuil, 1957. (In English: *The Divine Milieu*. New York: Harper Perennial Modern Classics, 2001.)

Church, R. *The Voyage Home*. Cited in E. Jacques. "Morte e crisi di mezza età," In *L'età di mezzo*. Edited by E. Jacques, O. F. Kernberg, and C. M. Thompson. Turin: Bollati Boringhieri, 1993.

Clément, O. *Dialogues avec le patriarche Athénagoras*. Paris: Fayard, 1969.

Davy, M.-M. *La connaissance de soi.* Paris: PUF, 1966.

Dossetti, G. "L'esperienza religiosa: testimonianza di un monaco," in Burgalassi Bausola et al., *L'Esperienza religiosa oggi.* Milan: Vita e Pensiero, 1986.

Elias, N. *La solitudine del morente.* Bologna: Il Mulino, 1985.

Flipo, C. "Et les jeunes: l'apprentissage de l'amour." *Christus,* April 1992.

Fromm, E. *La rivoluzione della speranza.* Milan, 1978.

Illich, I. *Nemesi medica: L'espropriazione della salute.* Milan: Mondadori, 1977.

Jabès, E. *Le Soupçon, le Désert.* Paris: Gallimard, 1978.

Jacques, F. "La promesse et le pardon." *Archivio di Filosofia* 1/3 (1987).

Jankélévitch, V. *Traité des Vertus.* Vol. 2, *Les Vertus et l'amour.* Paris/Montreal: Bordas, 1970.

Jung, C. In Zumkeller 1994.

Jüngel, E. *La pazienza di Dio e dell'uomo.* Brescia: Morcelliana, 1985.

———. *Morte.* Brescia: Queriniana, 1972.

Leclercq, J. *Cultura umanistica e desiderio di Dio.* Florence: Sansoni, 1965.

Le Saux, H. *Initiation à la spiritualité des Upanishads: Vers l'autre rive.* Sisteron: Présence, 1979.

Lochet, L. "Au service des malades: l'Union catholique des malades." In *La Vie Spirituelle* 353, 1950.

Lowen, A. *Il narcisismo: l'identità rinnegata.* Milan: Euroclub, 1986.

Mancini, R. *Comunicazione come ecumene: il significato antropologico e teologico dell'etica comunicativa.* Brescia: Queriniana, 1991.

Marcel, G. *Homo Viator: Prolegomeni ad una metafisica della speranza.* Turin: Borla, 1967.

Mollat, D. "Saint Jean l'Evangéliste." *Dictionnaire de Spiritualité*. Vol. 8, col. 224. Paris: Beauchesne, 1974.

Ott, H. *La Preghiera: linguaggio dell'uomo*. Genoa: Marietti, 1991.

Péguy, C. *Men and Saints*. New York, 1944. In Adorno 1994.

Ratzinger, J. *La Chiesa: Una comunità sempre in cammino*. Balsamo: Paoline, 1991.

Rilke, R. M. *Lettere a un giovane poeta*. Venice: La Locusta, 1979. (In English: *Letters to a Young Poet*. New York: W.W. Norton & Company, 1993.)

Schuchardt, E. *Warum gerade ich? Leiden und glauben*. Frankfurt: Offenbach, 1990.

Sontag, S. *Interpretazioni Tendenziose*. Turin: Einaudi, 1975.

Watzalawick, P., J. H. Beavin, and D. D. Jackson, eds. *Pragmatica della comunicazione umana*. Rome: Astrolabrio, 1971.

Weil, S. *Attente de Dieu*. Paris: Fayard (Poche), 1966. (In English: *Waiting for God*. New York: Harper Perennial Modern Classics, 2009.)

———. *La pesanteur et la grâce*. Paris: Union Générale d'Editions, 1962. (In English: *Gravity and Grace*. Lincoln, NE: Bison Books, 1997.)

Zumkeller, S. "Vieillir et s'accomplir." *Sources* 4/5 (1994).

ABOUT PARACLETE PRESS
Who We Are

Paraclete Press is a publisher of books, recordings, and DVDs on Christian spirituality. Our publishing represents a full expression of Christian belief and practice—from Catholic to Evangelical, from Protestant to Orthodox.

We are the publishing arm of the Community of Jesus, an ecumenical monastic community in the Benedictine tradition. As such, we are uniquely positioned in the marketplace without connection to a large corporation and with informal relationships to many branches and denominations of faith.

What We Are Doing
Books

Paraclete publishes books that show the richness and depth of what it means to be Christian. Although Benedictine spirituality is at the heart of all that we do, we publish books that reflect the Christian experience across many cultures, time periods, and houses of worship. We publish books that nourish the vibrant life of the church and its people—books about spiritual practice, formation, history, ideas, and customs.

We have several different series, including the best-selling Paraclete Essentials and Paraclete Giants series of classic texts in contemporary English; Voices from the Monastery—men and women monastics writing about living a spiritual life today; award-winning poetry; best-selling gift books for children on the occasions of baptism and first communion; and the Active Prayer Series that brings creativity and liveliness to any life of prayer.

Recordings

From Gregorian chant to contemporary American choral works, our music recordings celebrate sacred choral music through the centuries. Paraclete distributes the recordings of the internationally acclaimed choir Gloriæ Dei Cantores, praised for their "rapt and fathomless spiritual intensity" by *American Record Guide*, and the Gloriæ Dei Cantores Schola, which specializes in the study and performance of Gregorian chant. Paraclete is also the exclusive North American distributor of the recordings of the Monastic Choir of St. Peter's Abbey in Solesmes, France, long considered to be a leading authority on Gregorian chant.

Videos

Our videos offer spiritual help, healing, and biblical guidance for life issues: grief and loss, marriage, forgiveness, anger management, facing death, and spiritual formation.

Learn more about us at our website: www.paracletepress.com, or call us toll-free at 1-800-451-5006.

SCAN TO READ MORE

You may also be interested in other Voices from the Monastery ....

Strangers to the City

MICHAEL CASEY

ISBN: 978-1-61261-397-0; $15.99 Paperback

Eloquent and incisive, Casey invites you to embrace the challenge of gospel living that is opposed to the dominant, secular culture.

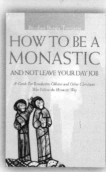

How to Be a Monastic and Not Leave Your Day Job

BR. BENET TVEDTEN

ISBN: 978-1-61261-414-4; $14.99, Paperback

This essential guide explains how people who live and work in "the world" are still invited to balance work with prayer, cultivate interdependence with others, practice hospitality, and otherwise practice their spirituality like monks.

Faith Can Give Us Wings

NOTKER WOLF

ISBN: 978-1-61261-303-1; $15.99, Paperback

A relationship with God, Wolf explains, can feel like falling in love. Beauty, joy, belief, trust, and forgiveness can show how it is possible to have wings of faith—and fly!

Available from most booksellers or through Paraclete Press:
www.paracletepress.com • 1-800-451-5006
Try your local bookstore first.